Second Career Volunteer,

a passionate, pennywise approach to a unique lifestyle

Barbara M. Traynor

authorHOUSE®

AuthorHouse™
1663 Liberty Drive
Bloomington, IN 47403
www.authorhouse.com
Phone: 1-800-839-8640

Published by AuthorHouse 4/25/2012

ISBN: 978-1-4685-7974-1 (hc)
ISBN: 978-1-4685-7973-4 (e)
ISBN: 978-1-4685-7975-8 (sc)

Library of Congress Control Number: 2012906502

To George

Acknowledgment

I acknowledge the fact that I could not continue my lifestyle without the support and love of my family.

I acknowledge the compassionate network of my writer friends, along with their dedication to the craft of writing.

I acknowledge a special group of dedicated volunteer friends accumulated one-by-one from the moment I joined this special word-of-mouth Network.

I acknowledge the organizations that offer the opportunity to get-out-and-give-back to all who wish to serve the greater good.

I acknowledge that, despite the drama and trauma, *life is good.*

Contents

Introduction

Find your Route 66

Change happens. However, when something as predictable as a book's targeted audience expands to encompass unexpected interested parties, it must be acknowledged.

When I first heard about volunteering with organizations that offer *free* room and board in exchange for workplace skills, I followed my instincts. This became a deliberate year-long action. Over the past six years, day by day, while volunteering and while sharing my experiences at various book events, I came to realize that what I had discovered is appropriate for pre and post retirees, Boomers, the unemployed, and college graduates and/or students taking a "decision-making-break". This prompted a twist on the original title to: ***Second Career Volunteer, a passionate, pennywise approach to a unique lifestyle***. The word lifestyle equates to living your life in a distinct manner. That manner is called *verve!* Since room and board is free in exchange for workplace skills, students can volunteer, adding this experience to their resume while investigating a precarious job market. And, a distinct plus, they can be independent; do not have to live at home with Mom and Dad. Even the unemployed have options. At a book event in Albuquerque a thirty-something said, "This in an investment in me. I've been unemployed for over a year. This volunteer option may lead to a real job!" I hope it did.

I now describe my volunteer lifestyle as silly putty. It is creative and can be stretched or compressed to fit your schedule. YOU are the one who speaks with a Volunteer Coordinator. YOU set the parameters that eventually fit into the organization of YOUR choice. YOU arrange the when, where, what, and how. Use your imagination. On your next vacation, stop by one of the organizations listed in the A-Z Index in the back of this book. Speak with the Volunteer Coordinator. Speak with the volunteers. Students, contact your Career Center about volunteering, garnering life experience prior to entering the workforce. Investigate. Research.

When people began traveling Route 66, they thought they were simply taking a ride. They could not have imagined what the road would become. That's how I feel about my lifestyle.

Get out, give back, enjoy

ONE:

Drama & Trauma

> *"It is not what we do, but what we do not do, for which we are accountable."*
>
> Molliere

Dropping straight down through Western Canada, to the east of Juneau, Alaska, is the almost paved Cassiar Highway. The road is drivable, unless it is raining and slick mud eases the car off into the wild. I'm driving alone on a clear day in August, windows down, slowly traversing the gravelly surface. My eyes are eager for dramatic jade hued lakes displayed in a setting of deep green foliage and my ears sensitive to the whistles of soaring eagles, when I hear a scratching sound. Glancing through the passenger window, I see a light brown lump rhythmically pouncing and pawing at the bark of a downed tree. A bear was looking for lunch! Easing the car into park, I watch for a while, snapping pictures from inside the car. Preparing to snap another, I realize the only sound is my idling engine. The bear has stopped scratching. Deliberately, he turns his head in my direction, rising to full height as only a grizzly can. I decide to drive on.

Driving to Alaska was a fantasy right up there with pigs flying! My reality was working as an administrative assistant for over forty-five years, raising three children as a single mother, circumstance generating abundant determination... and few resources. Yet, the concept of spending my first year of retirement as a volunteer in Alaska would evolve and, like the pigs, sprout wings to become a series of courageous adventures.

Life, like history, is cyclical. We are born into a predisposed lifestyle shaped by circumstance; we marry and produce children; they marry and the

1

cycle continues. We struggle to maintain control, blending compromise with perpetual adjustment to transition, be it childhood, college or employment. Our transitions ebb and flow. Some of us seem to experience more transition than others.

Over a twenty-year span, due to a grass-is-greener-spouse, I moved eighteen times across the country and back. Pioneering into the unknown can cause frustration and anxiety, but it also builds skills in how to deal with transition

Approaching retirement as just another transition is perhaps why my choice of a unique volunteer retirement lifestyle did not cause trepidation. I was accustomed to the drama and trauma of perpetual motion. Being a pioneer is not a new experience. However, becoming a role model was.

I never imagined retiring and volunteering in Alaska. It happened, spurred by circumstance, just like many of my other moves. But, unlike the previous random, frenzied relocations, this opportunity would prove to be positive and methodical. My adventure started when I received an e-mail from my sister telling me that while she and her husband were touring the Inside Passage of Alaska in their RV, they stopped to investigate Sitka.

Looking for a place to hook-up, they discovered Sheldon Jackson College, a small independent college that supplemented their staff with volunteers, offering room and board. Remembering that I mentioned hoping to travel in retirement my sister e-mailed the address of the volunteer coordinator. Since I would depend solely on Social Security income, the fact that the college provided room and board in return for working a forty hour week was crucial. I would only be responsible for transportation and incidental expenses. In other words, I only had to get there!

Like most women born around the end of WWII, I was raised to consider others before self. Today it seems self comes first—not selfish, self, as in responsibility to self before assuming responsibility for someone else. This outlook is focused on reality; more positive than negative. When thirty-somethings refer to their lifestyle, the reference is to "I" and "my" rather than "our". I began to reprogram myself to look at the rest of my life from this divergent perspective.

And, I am not alone. Boomers are another group discovering adjustments to lifestyle may be in order. Senior years are now the mystery of the future, a time when twenty-years or more can be anticipated, provided we are physically, emotionally, and financially prepared.

A Blessing of Smudge

Living far away from family for a year would be a new experience. Since I had been a presence in my grandchildren's lives for many years, preserving that loving relationship became paramount. To minimize the impending separation, and without being morose, I composed a poem, sharing my feelings about the opportunity of volunteering in Alaska, expressing my love for each child and reviewing past adventures we shared. I purchased two animal themed throws and, in Native American tradition, smudged each with sage, the smoke emitting the familiarity of scent and affection to replenish memories when called upon. This token, offered with love, mellowed my departure. I truly believe this gift softened the impending separation.

Retirement now translates to a time of independent imagination... independent of children, spouse (perhaps), job and/or responsibility. It is a coming of age shift in perception translating to "it's my turn and it's not selfish to admit it". Retirement is a time to reclaim dreams, a time to let passion fuel the ability to enjoy the rest of our lives, a time to get out of the "no" zone (no I can't; no, not right now, maybe later) into the "know" zone (I know I can). Contrary to popular belief, seventy is not the new fifty, it is the new seventy. Perhaps it is time to ask, what shall I do with these mystery years?

Life is not meant to be an obstacle course, although we deal with obstacles constantly disguised as day-to-day issues. Managing the drama and trauma of daily life with a positive attitude should be a priority. While where and how we live can and does influence any decision we make, it is how that decision feels that counts. Analyze it. Is the decision made through want or need? Before anticipation blends want and need into gray, focus on a retirement plan that includes most or all of the dreamed of wants.

The retirement pattern we see today developed gradually over the last century. Fluctuating labor markets and corrupted pension incomes explain why some opt for retirement, irrespective of Social Security parameters. Workaholics are tenacious, but others face an early exit because of age, illness, or changes in management. The recent financial crisis caused monumental cutbacks in staff and inventory, leading to massive unemployment. In addition, the decline in agriculture and the lure of leisure options tempt some to ignore the morning alarm. Bank accounts have deflated along with diminished 401k's. Shades of the late 20's depression.

Americans are known to take the shortest vacations in the industrialized world. We often live our work, disregarding the importance of unstructured recreation. No wonder the idea of unlimited time is enticing.

Still, the concept of retirement often strikes fear and trepidation. Faced with financial insecurity, we feel we might not be able to afford food, much less travel. The past influences the present. Depending on social and economic environments, the first fifty years of life was probably driven by random, decisive choices made at a time of indecision, expectations adjusted for disparate reasons. Most of us muddled through, achieving success or not.

When considering retirement reorganize priorities, alter the blueprint, and develop a plan. I conceived my plan while walking on the beach one wintry afternoon. My decision was to volunteer somewhere else. Choosing to live and volunteer locally would have meant status quo, something I wished to change.

Investigate how your lifestyle fits into the "Five Stages of Retirement,"[1] explained in detail in Chapter 2. Each interview will contain these stages (also see Appendix #1).

People of all ages and backgrounds, including seniors, are choosing to diversify their short-term local volunteerism by accepting long-term volunteer responsibilities in other states, and in some instances, countries. College students are considering volunteering *before* entering the workplace. This enhances local and long-distance opportunities. The world can change for the better, both at home and abroad by utilizing workplace skills. I feel long-term long-distance volunteering is the best of both worlds.

My children, after expressing cautions regarding safety, championed my decision. Friends were curious. Men (mostly) were surprised that I would drive solo, yes, even the thirty-somethings. Women asked questions, probing for information as to when, why, and how. Enthusiastic about my

---

1   Comprehensive retirement study, Ameriprise Financial, Age Wave & Ken Dychtwalk, Ph.D., Harris Interactive, Inc. January, 2006

new lifestyle, I probably told them far more than they needed to hear, but when planning something unique, the spirit of the moment is infectious!

How to Transition
- *A to-do list is KEY!*
- *Resign your job or make it digital.*
- *Change your footprint! Sell or readjust current housing.*
- *Downsize possessions.*

After transitioning with ease, I would drive off into the sunset, right? Yes, almost that easy. Though every transition contains obstacles, issues and decisions, most can be overcome. Prioritize. Ask family and friends to help move and store. This way, TO-DO LIST items will be completed one-by-one. Goodbyes may hold a tear or two, but celebration parties will be joyous.

From start to finish, preparing for my volunteer retirement lifestyle took an entire year because I made time for focused, logical, and prudent planning. As a single female, I rejoiced, content with my decisions. My retirement date was mid-July and by early summer, my exciting experience was imminent. Of course, if "I" is "we", plans may be a bit more bilateral.

Being single does simplify retirement. Certainly, there is a financial advantage—only one person to feed, house, and entertain—but, what about the joy of sharing? Couples may argue that being single is defined as being alone. However, singles may define alone as being independent and free.

Being single, sixty-five, and healthy is a distinct advantage. I chose to focus this book on fixed-income retirees (probably) sixty-five plus, couples or single, most of who must wait for the maximum Social Security payment before leaving salaried employment with health benefits. Considering the recent financial crisis, this group (along with some Boomers) is actively searching for options. Alternative lifestyles that supplement Social Security income and Medicare health coverage are essential to a financially deprived retiree's well-being.

Again, the focus of this book is to retirees, and it still is, for the most part. However, since the unemployed and college graduates may also take advantage of the option for long-term, long-distance volunteering, you will read references to them.

Studies verify that between the age of sixty and seventy, married or single, major changes interrupt the lives of seniors. A spouse may die, a prospective retiree may be pressed into becoming a caregiver for a partner or aged parents or young grandchildren, retirement savings may vanish. Any number of planned or unplanned events may occur.

In this age of technology, it is essential to guard against isolation. Laptops are essential for communication, but be aware that spending too many hours glued to your PC may lead to isolation. To fill retirement hours, or if social contacts are limited and/or a decision is made to relocate to a new environment, make a point to visit the numerous Senior Centers located in most cities and towns. Activities are listed on a bulletin board or newsletter. Sign up to volunteer locally as a way to meet friends with common interests. Visit the local library. Many pleasant conversations take place in the reading room, at social functions (usually free), or simply while perusing the bookshelves. Check out the list of book clubs, lectures and activities, perhaps some will appeal or even match a particular talent.

For additional income and as a way to meet people, look for part-time work. Even if only for five or ten hours, a part-time job can supplement income and enlarge a circle of friends. My fixed income is a fact. It is my choice to be realistic about finances.

On the issue of single men retirees vs. single women, single men are at a disadvantage regardless of being in demand through gender longevity. This simply means that as the population ages, women tend to live longer and healthier than men, leading to disproportionate numbers. Although retirement living complexes usually show men and women enjoying various activities, the reality is there are always more women at functions than men. This disproportion may be a factor when making decisions.

Morale: if a woman is looking for a partner to share later years, check out the demographics first!

Tip Before Leaving Before leaving for any long-distance volunteer assignment, complete a Temporary Change of Address card at the local Post Office, with start and stop designation. Mail will follow.

Retirement is an adult playground with a see-saw. The ride will be sometimes up, sometimes down. Therefore, as with any new endeavor, a successful retirement does involve psychological and physical cooperation. To survive this unknown playground, breathe into a 70s state of mind. Freedom, baby! Realize that limits are self-imposed.

Whether alone or with a partner, get up and dressed in the morning. Make a call to meet someone for a walk in the park. Try the new coffeehouse for lunch or a cold drink, rent a movie for the evening and invite someone over to share the experience. Streamed movies and library DVD's are economical, varied and accessible. Read that book for the Book Club that will meet next week and of course, volunteer. Weather and illness may hold you back, but most days mature adult should be out and about. Breathe into the positives.

One aspect of retirement which cannot be ignored is financial. There are many ways to economize within the community such as taking the bus or walking instead of driving. Of course, this assumes health is optimal but if not, Senior Centers do provide transportation to and from events, shopping, even doctor appointments. If long-distance travel is desired, there will be costs involved. I planned for this in my budget. Driving alone is the ultimate in freedom, but there is the bus or train. Details of travel and expenses are interspersed through the book.

Nuts and Bolts for Driving to a Volunteer Destination:

- *A large trunk!: Driving allows latitude in packing. There is room for personal preferences like flannel sheets and toiletries; remote destinations sometimes mean higher prices. Plan accordingly.*
- *Car maintenance: Schedule a tune up and/or oil change, check tires. If this is financially daunting, suggest a holiday or birthday gift card. Review car insurance and notify agent if anticipating a lengthy period of time away.*
- *Waterproof jacket: Sitka, Alaska is smack in the middle of a temperate rain forest. Invest in necessary items for your destination. Be frugal.*
- *Cell phone for emergencies: This item is personal and subject to desire/style, fees and conditions. Be prudent. Investigate whether or not calling cards or a renewable-minute phone would be more suitable? Designate foreign or domestic use.*

- *Laptop for wireless access: I purchased mine prior to retirement. Seniors with laptops are commonplace. Don't own one? Libraries offer WIFI free or for a small fee. So do coffee houses and restaurants.*

During my transition into my *mystery* years, maps and ideas were in my mind, on the floor, and on the dining room table. To forestall anxiety and keep the condo ready for prospective buyers, I organized copious research into a travel binder nicknamed "co-pilot". Purchase or recycle a large five-inch, three-ringed binder capable of withstanding much handling that will hold notes, reservation confirmations, and maps in non-glare plastic sleeves. Mapping websites are available 24/7 to help plot a trip with mileage, time and directions. Invest in an auto emergency card. Internet travel information is accessible and invaluable. The only adverse (but pleasant) challenge is finding time to visit all the desired landmarks. Once compiled, my binder resided, open, in the passenger seat for convenient viewing. Such a marvelous companion—never talked back!

The options for routes to Alaska were numerous, governed only by time constraints. In retirement most dream of Paris or the South Seas. My wish is to visit and hike our national parks. Driving to Alaska, I was able to visit four national parks in the U.S. and Canada; the return trip, which took seven leisurely weeks, allowed me to sightsee and hike in at least eight more.

Overnight stays were with family, friends, or at inexpensive hotels. As an afterthought, I queried local newspapers suggesting I write a travel journal for their reader's enjoyment (and income for me). One editor thought "the idea of a woman driving alone across the Continental Divide" would be fascinating, and asked that I e-mail an accounting of my experiences. Great! I try to take advantage of every financial opportunity.

With giddy anticipation, I was ready. What began as imagination had evolved to a leap of faith. Bearing no resemblance to, but feeling like Joan of Arc, I drove out of the driveway to begin my great adventure.

Eight-thousand miles is a long drive! The pleasure of setting my own schedule and the comfort of a personalized itinerary made it enjoyable. Yes, there were planned stops for rest and oil changes, but the clock was ticking. I needed to reach Prince Rupert to board my designated Alaskan Marine Highway ferry on schedule.

With that in mind, the first leg of my journey took me through Denver, Colorado. From Denver, I drove North through the Rockies, past the Great Salt Lake into Canada, up the Icefields Parkway, turning left at Jasper heading West to Prince Rupert, British Columbia. At the appointed hour, I drove my car (with a variety of other cars, trucks, RV's, school busses and bicycles) onto the Alaskan Marine Highway ferry for an invigorating two-night trip through some of the most dramatic scenery I've ever seen.

On the ferry, we traveled north past the mammoth blue-tinged Mendenhall Glacier to dock at Juneau, a gull squawking, eagle swooping, industrious port to exchange passengers and supplies. Speaking with my fellow travelers, I learned that the ferry system is the most affordable land link for goods.

Along the Way .... *Alaskan Marine Highway ferries are built to traverse shallow Alaskan waters. We would proceed through the Wrangell Narrows north to Juneau, passengers boarding and embarking at various stops on our way to Sitka. Our Captain invited all to witness the unique navigational experience of the Narrows at 14:00 hours (2 a.m.). Not wishing to make a night-time announcement, he advised those interested to set an alarm. I did not book a cabin, opting to sleep on the covered deck with others in sleeping bags and tents, so at the appointed hour with the assistance of my vibrating cell phone alarm, I quietly climbed over snoozing passengers and made my way down to the rail. Since navigation is governed by the tide, not by the hour, the Narrows boasts a series of warning lights dictating course. What a spectacular sight! I stared at the display, red and green lights stretched like an elongated horizontal Christmas tree guiding our ferry. We were told that fog might obscure—not so. I watched until the lights disappeared into the blackness. Grateful and sleepy, I slipped back into my deck chair to dream of what greater experiences lay ahead.*

Making a "U" turn around the top of Baranoff Island, our ferry cruised south to Sitka among sleek grey whales breeching in the aquamarine waters. Scraggy groups of brown otters munched on kelp while cameras clicked and passengers pointed, adults shrieking right along with the children. We docked in Sitka on a warm and sunny August afternoon. I grinned. Finally, Alaska!

Driving by instinct and somewhat distracted by my surroundings, I approached the single stop-light in the center of town with trepidation. Directly in front of me, boats bounced on the sapphire waters of Sitka Harbor. By the way, Sitka boasts only fourteen miles of paved road; the Volunteer Coordinator discouraged bringing a car. Only after I described my anticipated cross-country trip, did she relent, stating that "You will not drive much once you've arrived". Hmmm... I observed. Perhaps not, since all the action seemed to be centered near the Harbor.

My assigned volunteer position at the college was for forty-hours a week as administrative assistant in the business office. While my responsibilities were demanding, evenings and weekends were free for hiking, kayaking, and socializing. There were long spring and summer daylight hours to investigate mountain switchbacks and lazy trails with fellow volunteers. Evenings found us peering at eagles teaching their young how to hunt. I crammed all that I could into every available minute meeting townspeople, having dinner at the tribal hall, enjoying salmon, halibut and herring egg salad (a local culinary delight), experiencing the drumming and dancing. I absorbed Tlingit folklore and listened to tales of Alaskan fishing. I toured Russian landmarks by attending local celebrations, lectures and festivities, exploring every inch of drivable road.

On Alaska Day, most volunteers from the college dressed as Russian soldiers to march in the parade and partake in the flag ceremony reenactment. Castle Hill in Sitka is where the United States formally took possession of the territory of Alaska. Sitka boasts an abundance of Russian and Tlingit history, many talented musicians, and a passionate association with the sea. Lives are dictated by the salmon and herring spawning.

Fall and winter passed quickly, including the "dark time", a depressing stretch of time from October to February when daylight happened from 9:00 a.m. to 3:00 p.m. Sitka residents fill these days with musical entertainment, basketball and assorted imaginative activity. I would search the newspaper looking for opportunities, so much so that I earned the name "Activity Director". There was much to see and learn, but it was already May, and my first opportunity of volunteering in retirement would soon be at an end.

When friends realized I would be gone for an entire year, they questioned why a year, why not a shorter first-time stint? To savor the entire experience

and to justify the distance driven, a year seemed right. I stand on that decision.

While volunteering in Sitka, I explored the Inside Passage of Alaska ferried to Kodiak Island (off-season), and hiked Mt. Edgecombe, a fourteen mile trek accessible only by boat. Such an exciting, memorable year, and too soon it was time to return to the Northeast. Some of my fellow volunteers came and went, time served according to their needs, but I experienced an entire cycle of seasons. With every departure there were tears and smiles. We remain in contact, visiting as we travel to volunteer destinations throughout the country. Perhaps one day, I will return.

During my journey back and upon arrival in the Northeast, those I spoke with marveled at my experiences and distance traveled. In the course of living my volunteer retirement lifestyle, I became an accidental role model, pointed to as an example of independence and courage. My daughter's friends joke, referring to me as Waldo, asking "where is your mother now?" One acquaintance, dissatisfied with her current commute, changed her priorities and job, not retiring, but restructuring her life and attitude in the process.

Another friend did retire, achieving her elusive goal of Foreign Service. Previously she considered her finances inadequate, but told me, "If you can, I can!" She is now volunteering in Honduras.

To research volunteer opportunities, peruse the A-Z web address listings with brief descriptions in the back of this book, or begin by typing the word "volunteer" in the address line on the Internet. The options are numerous. It will take time and effort, so be prepared to spend more than a few hours investigating particular interests to match specific lifestyle needs.

While in Arkansas, a fellow volunteer confided: "Yup, in a few months I enter into what is called the 'senior years of life'." She laughed, "I say to those who look at our volunteer lifestyle and want it, that they need to think about their future and create a way of planning for it. How do we want to live life? As far as I am concerned, the unknown awaits."

Another friend told me that taking a chance on an unknown lifestyle took verve. I looked it up. Verve means possessing a special ability to pull something off with panache and wild, chaotic, unpredictable passion. It is the abandonment of reason in the reckless pursuit of pleasure, no matter how outrageous. Although I am cautious and methodic in my planning, my demeanor probably exuded verve with a capitol "V". Every now and then I recommend experiencing verve.

Explore every opportunity. Do remember, though that overconfidence and independence may lead to the false assumption that negativity will not rear its ugly head. Be cautious, but always curious. When taking that first leap into a volunteer retirement lifestyle, be happy with your decision. Make certain that Social Security is scheduled for direct deposit, ATM and Medicare cards are in a safe place, a digital camera is handy for pictures, and cell phone charged.

Go for it!

Frequently Asked Questions

*1. **Did you drive an SUV?** No. My Chevrolet sedan is ten-years old. Before leaving the car was serviced, belts and tires checked. On the road, I scheduled oil changes into my itinerary. Maintenance is imperative. Defensive driving, along with security precautions are important. ALWAYS LOCK YOUR CAR.*

*2. **I am anxious about driving alone. How did you manage the isolation and fear?** It helps to be psychologically independent, accustomed to initiating travel experiences. Investigate hostels. I was never completely alone. My blue binder "co-pilot" sat alongside and my cell phone was always charged. Limiting day driving to five or six hours also helped. I seldom experienced and anxiety. I was too busy enjoying! Try enticing another volunteer to join your journey, to share the experience. Remember, driving solo is not a prerequisite to long-distance volunteering. There are many alternative ways to travel.*

*3. **You mention college students - why?** College graduates are entering a volatile workplace, perhaps non-existent. Volunteering is a budgetary option during that transition. Retirees are not the only people who can volunteer.*

*4. **What qualities are a must for success in the volunteer world?** PATIENCE, FLEXIBILITY, and COMROMISE! And of course, the old standby: don't take anything personally.*

Interview: Clarissa

Mesa Verde Cliff Dwellings

Clarissa ... *mother, daughter, teacher, librarian, volunteer and clever Scrabble player.*

Clarissa loves the high desert country and native culture. She searched the Internet for specific volunteering criteria and found the National Park site. There were two places—Mesa Verde and the Grand Canyon. We spoke of volunteer experiences when she visited the Heifer Ranch in Arkansas (while I was volunteering there) and through frequent cell phone calls.

"Mesa Verde needed a librarian for the winter months," Clarissa said, "and they offered a private house plus some funding for food. The Grand Canyon offered a library tech position with housing in a shared two bedroom trailer and additional monies for food. I chose the Mesa Verde National Park," she continued, "since the position available was for a Librarian and they offered the opportunity to increase my knowledge of the Ancient Puebloans. Perfect!"

Why Clarissa volunteers .... *"I feel I have received so much from so many people that it was time to pass on the good works. I could now afford not to be* *paid for my skills, but to simply offer them to others. My children were finally old enough that I could leave for extended periods. Also, I felt there were many people hurting emotionally in the world, and perhaps I could be of some help."*

Since her home in North Carolina is rather hot and humid in the summer, Clarissa prefers to volunteer where the humidity is low, and areas like the high desert take priority. Because she chose a volunteer retirement lifestyle, she is in control of responsibilities, hours, destination, and choice of climate.

"I really enjoyed my experience at Mesa Verde," she said, "and I guess they did too, because they invited me to apply for a temporary job as a summer librarian."

Clarissa was not always a librarian. She began her career as a music teacher. "As a band and orchestra director, I had great fun teaching music and encouraging the children to love music. Our band contest ratings increased by three levels, I was particularly proud that our school orchestra featured more string soloists than most schools, and as if that wasn't enough, the combined fourth grade classes presented an operetta!"

This was not a boast, rather insight into the life of a dedicated woman who loves working with children and puts full effort into all tasks. After teaching for a while, Clarissa realized that directing the band and orchestra alone did not fit her ultimate goals.

In 1967, she returned to school to obtain a master's degree in library science, and began her career as a medical librarian. For twenty-five years she enjoyed this rewarding, enjoyable career, which as it happens, was a precursor to the future. Before and during her library career, she and her family relocated a few times, moving from Louisiana to Florida, and then to North Carolina where Clarissa took a position as an administrative librarian at Western Carolina University in Cullowhee. This felt like home. Six years later, in 2003, with the children grown or in college, she decided to retire at age sixty-two.

"My decision to retire early is something I do not regret," she stated. "I highly recommend it to anyone. Because I chose to delay my Social Security payments until full-payment eligibility, things were a little tight, but it turned out to be the best plan for me. It allowed me the ability to be on my own schedule while reserving my maximum income for later."

After her retirement, Clarissa once again decided to try something new and enrolled in a program to become a lay minister. However after two years of study, she did not feel called to serve in a church.. "At this point," she said with a laugh, "that darn old foot started itchin' and I became eager to hit the mission path."

Realizing there may be places in the U.S. that could use volunteer help, her thoughts turned to the West and Alaska —places only dreamed of. "My father deserves the credit for my itchy foot," Clarissa explained, "along with my love of travel plus the desire to investigate and experience new things."

She went online and up popped Sheldon Jackson College in Sitka , Alaska.

"Great," she thought, "they offer room and board. All I have to do is get there." She wondered what her mission would be, and soon found herself volunteering in the nursery at the day care center. "Wonderful place," she said enthusiastically. "I got to play with the babies, and experience a totally different culture. Sure, some days the children were cranky and my back hurt, but they are so vulnerable and adorable. I also made three lifelong friends, all in five short months. Pretty good, huh?"

In Sitka, Clarissa chose to attend one of the many local churches and became involved with ministering to others and being ministered to. She also formed close friendships with the women who resided in the single women's volunteer housing.

"We went everywhere together. We cooked, cleaned and looked after one another," she said and quickly added, "Now, don't make it seem all that selfless. Shared housing is give and take, a kind of reciprocal ministry that is if playing Scrabble and working jigsaw puzzles could be called ministry."

Cause and effect: Each volunteer position is different. Volunteer organizations solicit skilled retirees because they do not have an adequate budget for payroll. Occasionally, because of limited funding, facilities may need maintenance, services may be lacking, or the position applied for is misrepresented. A volunteer may run into difficult, even intolerable, situations. Before, during and after you commit to offering your services, if a negative situation occurs, find someone to speak with and work it out. If this cannot happen, there are other places to investigate, other responsibilities to assume. Volunteering, like life, may not always go smoothly.

It is the reciprocal connection, the thread that connects all volunteers that she feels is most important. This type of interaction should not be taken for granted since it does not happen everywhere she volunteers. Clarissa is grateful when it does. "While sharing with others," she says, "it is evident that life experiences have their effect. This sense of community is the essence of my volunteer retirement life."

After Sitka, Clarissa returned home to North Carolina for three months to get reacquainted with family and friends, but soon the "itchy foot syndrome" cropped up again. This time, to experience a totally new culture, she chose New Mexico . At Ghost Ranch, a Presbyterian Conference Center near Abiquiu, Clarissa utilized her educational and organizational skills while developing museum guides for visitors and worksheets for school children. In addition, she put her retail sales skills to use in the Conference Center gift shop.

While performing her volunteer responsibilities at Ghost Ranch, Clarissa continued her interest in Native American farming techniques and the uses of native plants. As with most indigenous cultures, she found that plants were used for both food and medicine.

"It is great to learn that many contemporary medicines come from the native plants of this area," she said. "Because of my friendship with one Native American woman I got to learn about a native plant used for treating coughs and cold symptoms. My friend knew the medicine worked because her people used it for centuries!" This is just one example of how women of all cultures are able to connect.. While at Ghost Ranch, Clarissa made several excursions to out-of-the-way Indian ruins and pueblos.

Pueblo Research ... *The Ancient Puebloans were mostly farmers and gatherers. Around 600 A.D. Puebloans built pit houses—areas dug about 3 to 4 feet into the ground, timbers planted in each corner. The homes had head space of about 6 feet. They were without windows, but had a ventilator shaft and a hole in the roof. Around 700 A.D., they began to build pueblo type structures that were long, low and narrow. Then, around 1100 A.D., inhabitants moved into large stone alcoves under the edge of the mesa cliffs. These structures were three to four stories high and were very well built of stones. Puebloans still farmed the mesa tops and developed granaries for food storage.*

Completing her volunteer responsibilities New Mexico, she returned to North Carolina for five months. Clarissa proudly stated that her children are out on their own, responsible in their own right.

"I don't feel guilty like some do, about leaving my children to live their own lives," she offered, hesitating for a moment, "because they grow and so do I. My oldest son tells me that he is proud of my volunteering and travel. My children have kept me young at heart if not body, and are pleased that I have a busy, productive lifestyle." (Read more about family approval or disapproval in Chapter 5.)

Clarissa commented that the National Park Service, like other government agencies and organizations who offer volunteer positions, are under financial duress. Her personal assessment was that because Mesa Verde cannot afford to pay for a full time librarian, they make do with people who possess a love of books, which leads to inefficiency.

"Previous to my accepting the position at Mesa Verde," she confided, "they hired a professional librarian for a while, but since then the position of cataloger of new books has remained unfilled. I took on the additional responsibility of playing catch-up on cataloguing, besides my other duties of shelving, circulation, and assisting clients. I feel the most helpful thing I accomplished was to enable each workstation to access the entire library catalog."

Because of her work, clients may now access the catalog from the Library Homepage she implemented. From there, they can refer to guides she developed to aid them in their search.

"This type of work is extremely rewarding," she said, "but in addition, I am pleased that I was able to continue my research into the life and culture of the Ancient Puebloans."

Clarissa emphasized that all her volunteer experiences have been fun, educational, even exciting, and have not cost beyond transportation there and back. "For me, volunteering is the way to go. Sure, there may be negatives, but no matter where I go, a sense of mission is always with me. At the college in Sitka, I noticed two children at the daycare center who were not being appreciated as unique individuals. I just could not sit by and watch. It was important to me to say something, to take action."

It is up to the volunteer working within a given situation to determine what they can tolerate. Sometimes what will test one volunteer's limits will not matter to another.

Among her other skills, Clarissa is a weaver, and it sounds to me like some of the warp and weft is comprised of listening, compassion, and the ability to learn from her experiences. In her present position at Mesa Verde National Park, she enjoys a temporary position with a stipend. Life is good and she does not ask for more.

In a recent e-mail, Clarissa wrote: "It is a beautiful day, high about seventy and fluffy white clouds in a blue, blue sky." She described how, when returning from a hike by the river, she found her landlord sitting on the front porch playing his guitar and singing.

The week prior, she had visited the Dolores River Valley in Colorado. "It is just the most beautiful sight with the aspens budding in their lime green splendor, contrasted against the deeper dark hues of the evergreens. I took a side trip to Lizard Head Pass, altitude about 10,250 feet, with patches of snow here and there—just beautiful!"

What is ahead for Clarissa? Her plans are temporary, awaiting final decisions. Right now there is hiking by the river, a piece of cloth to weave, and all those stars to look at on a clear, clear night.

"I feel I am fortunate in my choice of varied experiences," she said. "It is up to the volunteer to make every experience unique." Note: Clarissa now resides in Colorado.

Clarissa's active participation in the Five Stages of Retirement:
1. **Imagination**—*upgrading an undergraduate degree into a Masters of Library Science, and acknowledging her thirst for travel;*
2. **Anticipation**—*working while looking forward to when her children would be grown and independent;*
3. **Liberation**—*"freedom to be on her own schedule;"*
4. **Transition**—*two year program to become a lay minister to counsel and help others;*
5. **Reconciliation**—*happiness in volunteering, contributing library and counseling skills.*

TWO:
Agin' is Changin'

> *"Don't be afraid to take big steps. You can't cross a chasm in two small jumps."* David Lloyd George, British Prime Minister (1863-1945)

Change happens. It can be as simple as grass growing or as profound as birth. Simple or profound, it is constant fluctuation. How we respond to this fluctuation in our immediate surroundings governs our attitude and inspires growth or indifference. This book is a prime example. The first edition appealed to retirees. This book presents options to all.

Above my computer is posted the following: Respond, don't react. Allowing time for response is a positive action. A knee-jerk reply is almost always negative. Hesitation, sometimes no longer than a single breath, is essential for turning a situation from negative to positive.

In our highly volatile world, change, whether self-initiated or naturally occurring, commands our attention. What happens when a pebble is dropped into a pool of water? The pebble sinks, but the ever widening ripples continue long after the pebble disappears from view.

From the moment of birth, life is a series of ripples, some inevitable, some not. Retirement is one of those inevitable changes. Endeavor to make it positive.

Top Ten Reasons to Retire
- *To be able to complete a task without interruption.*
- *To discover passions worth visiting or revisiting.*

Barbara M. Traynor

- *To respond to new opportunities with wisdom garnered through experiences in the workforce.*
- *To get up and out where and when you wish.*
- *To volunteer and encourage others to do the same.*
- *To enjoy the freedom to take a risk without the baggage of dependent children or elderly parents.*
- *To pursue learning experiences that in the past seemed frivolous.*
- *To realize dreams before it's too late.*
- *To enjoy family.*
- *Because I want to.*

If retirees were to analyze their lives, most would agree that some change is voluntary, like getting married or deciding to have fish instead of hamburgers for dinner. However, other changes are beyond our control, such as downsizing in the workplace, a sudden disability, or a fire at home. Either way, change is intrusive and disruptive, but with forethought, negatives can become positives.

While retirement may be inevitable, aging is involuntary. Squinting at wrinkles or a gray hair or two when approaching a milestone birthday is normal, but unless a health issue interferes, aging is taken for granted.

We notice it only when we glance in the mirror. Though we judge others by how they look, we judge ourselves by how we feel. A whole generation matures before you realize that the new office manager looks like a high school graduate. Ready or not, age fifty-five is the threshold to the senior years.

Society as a whole is aging. This phenomenon is causing change in politics, social interactions, and medical coverage. Presented with more flexibility and opportunity than our parents ever dreamed of, it would be logical to think that we, as mature adult, would be happy.

However, as age accelerates, attitudes fluctuate. A fervent desire to live life fully may be curtailed because of illness or stress, turning smiles to frowns. A while ago, I referred to this type of individual in a poem:

I spoke with a neighbor of mine yesterday
about . . "aging is changing . ."
... she snapped back to say,
"Now what do you mean? We're still getting old! ...
missing the point with her negative scold,
misplacing the blame for her ungraceful finish,
'til family and friends growing weary, diminish.

> *-Excerpt from The Pleasure of Aging author, Barbara M Traynor*

Some people are old at twenty, others young at eighty. Those who attended high school or college in the 1950s remember homes with bomb shelters, but without televisions, microwaves, personal computers, and cell phones.

All these conveniences are due to advances in technology. Long ago, I embraced technology and assimilated myself into this new age via on-the-job training. It was a matter of survival. Practicing daily at the keyboard, it became second-nature to enter data, marvel at the elimination of carbon paper, advance from the manual to the electric typewriter, to the personal computer.

Today, laptops are commonplace, cell phones ring in bathroom stalls, instant communication, instant news, instant macaroni and cheese. Most welcome innovation, although some are hesitant to accept the intrusion of technology, just as some were opposed to the Model-T or the Beatles. The main issue to avoid is isolation. We may wish to halt, postpone, or forestall change, but like the sunrise, change happens.

Think of how much positive and creative energy is wasted by resistance. Growth, if accepted with grace, is not painful. Change, like clay, is waiting to be molded into a personalized vessel. Take control of life, irrespective of its limitations. In the words of the English playwright George Bernard Shaw, "The people who get on in this world are the people who get up and look for the circumstances they want."

I mentioned earlier that our family moved eighteen times. Talk about change! I felt like a railroad engineer, hand poised to switch schools, switch jobs, switch in and out of relationships. The busy-ness I experienced changed my life from living to existing. When life is in constant turmoil, all of your energy goes into existing. Participation is superficial.

Life should not be a spectator sport. The person who chooses to live a purposeful life voluntarily participates in the future. No one knows how much time is allotted to accomplish goals, dreams, or possibilities. Participate fully in every aspect of impending or evolving retirement.

With significant increases in life expectancy, it is projected that retirement will last longer and longer. But you don't simply retire one day and wake up without an alarm the next. As with any change, retirement is a journey, a migration of stages through distinct emotions which impact our lives, along with the lives of family and friends.

The following five stages are meant as a guide to those emotions:

Five Stages of Retirement

1. **The First Stage—IMAGINATION:** *throughout our working lives we imagine possibilities. This is why we wake up at two in the morning with wishful thinking, dreams and daydreams.*

2. **The Second Stage—ANTICIPATION:** *This takes place just prior to retirement. Emotions intensify as the day approaches. This is a time of excitement and hope, but there are also feelings of worry and doubt, financial and social, and reaction to change.*

3. **The Third Stage—LIBERATION:** *This happens on the day of! We awaken enthused and full of hope. So begins the "honeymoon" phase.*

4. **The Fourth Stage—TRANSITION:** *This is a period of challenge as the retiree tries to adapt to a new lifestyle. A positive choice, carefully planned, will be joyful; if not, perhaps the challenges will outweigh the liberation. But sometimes desire overshadows reality, and liberation can be a two-edged sword.*

5. **The Fifth Stage—RECONCILIATION:** *The retiree has adapted to what is. This stage comes later, when contentment and acceptance become apparent.*

Each stage in retirement means change. The urge to counter the passing of time may manifest itself as a hurry-up-and-do-it-before-it-is-too-late feeling. Becoming older should be acknowledged as a meaningful and indispensable phase of life. Take a moment to reflect on those who did plan, but did not live to experience those plans for whatever reason. We may dismiss it as a cliché, but life really is short.

To prepare for the change of retirement, take a piece of paper and make a timeline with stages one through five, along with associated expectations. For guidelines, see the self-evaluation forms in the back of this book. Do not be tempted to discount the first stage since imagination and possibilities are still very relevant, even if retirement is imminent or you're already beyond retirement age. It is never too late to take the road less traveled.

Remember, retirement is a transition from a "job" to a "passion." For optimum results, the exercise of the Five Stages should be completed at least one year before retirement.

Examples:

- Susan did not realize that the imagination stage existed. She was too busy raising children, building a career, and struggling to get back on her feet after her divorce. She didn't have time for lunch, never mind anticipation. The transition from her divorce to single status may have resulted in a type of liberation, but not quite as described in Stage Three, and certainly not as a precursor to retirement. For Susan, retirement is now a goal. During the last five years, she has been cultivating part-time consultant opportunities, anticipating tending her garden, and considering downsizing to make independence in her own home a reality. When she does retire, Susan will transition into her retirement a little later than some, but with a plan that will reconcile her desires with her goals and objectives.

- Peter and Marjorie moved a few times while raising their family, always with an eye to upgrading financially. They imagined retirement as a time away from business pressures, free to do whatever they wished. There was barely time for anticipation since retirement came early in the form of a snap decision to purchase an RV. Within a few months, they had downsized and were on the road. With prudent decision-making and only a sketchy vision of what they intended to do, Social Security and a nest egg from real estate investments were sufficient to provide financial stability. Now liberated, they could begin their nomadic lifestyle. A transition of sorts came with learning to drive their RV and co-habit in close quarters with a very large dog. On their travels, they stopped to volunteer with Habitat for Humanity, joined with other nomad RV networks to assist on church projects, and took every opportunity to be hosts at National Parks. Reconciliation came in the form of freedom from constraints. "We come and go as we please," Marjorie said, "driving from one weather zone to another, matching our desires. We've built houses in Louisiana, hiked a desert in full-bloom in Arizona, taken time out to visit with our daughter in Seattle and help with renovations to her home. This would not have happened if we were locked into a permanent residence. In our RV, we've met so many people while working and playing. Perhaps, eventually, we will find a place to put down permanent roots, but not right now."

Yvonne *..teacher, wife, mother, volunteer Club President and team coordinator:*

"In the 1970's, a group of young women who had relocated to the Albany, New York area, including myself, were whining about the lack of social and cultural opportunities for young black professional women, so we got together to form the Black Women's Association of Albany. I served as President then, and have come full circle, once again elected to serve as the current President Our group gathers books and supplies for inner-city schools and contributes to Operation Christmas Child. We advocate for girls and women of color by raising scholarship monies, recognizing minority women who are community leaders during Women's History Month, and host an annual scholarship luncheon featuring prominent minority women speakers."

Yvonne has retired from teaching, but is still involved in the educational system as a substitute. In 2006, she attended a volunteer workshop offered in her area that featured Smartworks, a volunteer senior leadership program sponsored by Senior Services of Albany, New York. Yvonne teamed up with another volunteer to utilize her teaching and organizational skills for the Capital District United Way.

"The two of us were matched to initiate Managing Your Money work-shops, Yvonne said. "These programs would be offered to lower-income residents. We arranged for expert speakers, gathered informational hand-outs and provided

refreshments, all components that are part of a workshop. There were three presentations: 1. Credit Card Scams; 2. ID Theft; 3. Living Within a Budget. We all got something from that one. The United Way staff and project supervisor were so helpful and encouraging. It was a pleasure to work with them."

Yvonne credits the favorable outcome of the workshops to positive interaction throughout the project between Smartworks volunteers, the United Way and the residents. She enjoys volunteering within her community and will continue to do so.

Circumstance and attitude shape the future more often than not. At times, issues force reaction rather than response. However, planning does provide a positive base for retirement goals. It took me one entire year to plan my transition from employee into a volunteer retirement lifestyle.

What started with imagination blossomed into anticipation. Liberation occurred when I drove out of the driveway! My on-going volunteer retirement lifestyle did not become a reality until after my year in Alaska.

While there, during the transition stage, I found it was enjoyable to travel without the responsibility of permanent housing. Constant re-evaluation throughout that first year led to reconciliation, and an enjoyable retirement lifestyle. Excitement did provoke spontaneity, but it took deliberate cultivation to bring it to fruition.

Do not misunderstand, I love being spontaneous but do not go to extremes. Spontaneity works when choosing ice cream cone or what shirt to wear, but retirement represents a chunk of years that will be smoother with forethought.

Make time to experience the release, recovery, rejuvenation, and re-definition of retirement. Notice I said make not take. To make time implies a designated period set aside for an intended purpose, not a haphazard few minutes to jot down a few notes. Use the disorder of the past to chart a logical transition into the future.

Once plans and goals are completed, put them in a drawer and mark your calendar to review them in six months. Enjoy anticipating possibilities. Work at reprogramming outmoded mindsets so that you can actively participate in the future.

When it is time to review your plan, reflect on missed opportunities for enjoyment. Think about the times you postponed your desires to accommodate someone else's plans. How about all those procrastinations? Write them down so they will not happen again. Now is the time for your name to be first on the list.

Retiree Categories:

Empowered Re-inventor *(19%): looking forward to adventure, new challenges and fulfillment with substantial financial resources (think well-off Baby Boomers with reduced 401k's).*

Carefree Content *(19%): optimistic, but for them it is not a time of adventure. They are quite content with where they are at the present time, looking forward to not working as they feel they have saved for the future.*

Uncertain Searcher *(22%): positive or negative, no in-between. They are planning, but still attempting to reconcile goals and activities as finances may be shaky. Only 36% of those who retire have adequate resources.*

Worried Struggler *(40%): having the most difficult time. They have discounted planning, feeling resources are inadequate. Little thought has been given to retirement; they are taking it one day at a time.*

Think about the four groups of retirees. Are you empowered? Recognize a worried struggler? A little planning will ensure a happy, productive, and less stressful retirement than you ever imagined. My personal circumstance means that Social Security is my only income. If necessary, I can supplement it with part-time work because of my excellent health and marketable work skills. I plan every volunteering experience to mesh with scheduled time at home, so that if I need those few extra dollars, I am in familiar territory.

Ask yourself, what is my goal in retirement? Is it all about freedom from someone else's schedule? Is it travel? Is it a rocking chair? From the moment of birth we attempt to define who we are. Wasn't it the mantra of the 1960's to "find yourself"? Without a goal, we may find ourselves "worried strugglers."

What Are the Most Difficult Challenges in Retirement?

FIRST: Health care costs. Yes, really. Sometimes we don't take care of ourselves because of the costs involved. Most seniors on fixed incomes are stressed that the cost of insurance will force a decision between prescriptions and food.

SECOND: Money. Translation = having available spendable income. Most lower-income retirees depend on Social Security since their earnings during the working life did not permit savings. Lower-income retirees, especially women, are at the highest risk for poverty. Prepare a plan tailored to your financial limitations. If that vacation is a must, playing golf is important, or attending the symphony is a priority, suggest it to a family member for a holiday or birthday gift. A gift wish-list is appropriate for a change-of-lifestyle retiree. The most appreciated gifts are the ones you use today.

THIRD: Personality. Strange as it sounds, finances and health care costs are not the primary concern of some retirees. Personality is. Retirees vacillate between a change in lifestyle and maintaining the status quo. Retirement requires a leap of faith into the future. Flexibility is important, if not paramount. A rigid personality is detrimental to health.

Why Yvonne volunteers .... *"There is a feeling of satisfaction knowing you have made a difference," she says. "When I retired at age fifty-five, it was the first time I became involved with the elderly population, my parents' generation. Working with this community helped me to change my stereotypical attitude toward 'seniors'. One dynamic about Smartworks is that our project was more than stuffing envelopes. It required a fair amount of computer, organizational, and problem-solving skills. The Smartworks projects are meant to attract recently retired Boomers who still want to use their professional skills"* Yvonne and I agreed that using technological, educational or manual skills will be the salvation of many seniors, extending their productivity well beyond their years in the workforce. With the skilled workforce dwindling, senior volunteer retirees will be valuable assets to companies and organizations.

"In the 1980's we formed a group outside of school, the Capitol District Achievers. When it expanded we asked the YWCA for help and got a grant. To this day former students will come up to me and say, 'Remember when we did so-and-so?' Yvonne smiled. *" It is so gratifying to know I have made a difference."*

If you are unsure about any of these challenges some adjustment may be in order. Learning to be more economical takes a certain amount of patience and flexibility. There are many options for frugality if you are willing to revamp some old habits. Here are a few suggestions:

Books:

- *Free Stuff for Seniors* by Matthew Lesko, a syndicated columnist for The New York Times. It is chock full of common sense suggestions and should be available through local libraries. I did notice that when it was written the author listed his age as fifty. Currently, the official age of a senior is defined as fifty-five.

- *The Complete Tightwad Gazette*, by Amy Dacyczyn, 1998. This book is mostly advice for families with children, but it is still useful for mature adult. Some things, like dumpster diving, may not be for everyone, but most tips come in handy in this "penny-pincher's Bible."

- *Car Living Your Way*, by A.J. Heim. This is a realistic security-minded handbook describing the positives and negatives of living in your car; which may not appeal to everyone, however some volunteers do "live out of their car".

- *Volunteer Vacations Across America*, by Sheryl Kayne. This book is a resource designed to provide details on how to evaluate organizations, set a personal program and budget expenses. Check it out at the local library.

Travel:

- Hostels: When traveling, think hostel rather than hotel. Driving to Alaska, it annoyed me to pay $60 to $100 for a shower and a bed when it was only me and only for one night. To research hostels, Google "hostel" plus the city of your choice. Accommodations are not luxurious and may offer some inconveniences depending on your expectations. Most Internet sites are complete with pictures, comments, hours of operation, and 24/7 access for reservations. College students frequent hostels along with many foreign visitors. A great way to make new friends.

- Golden Pass: formerly known as the Golden Age Passport, allows those over 62 to enjoy traveling, camping, and sightseeing at U.S. national parks and recreation areas for free. Investigate the particulars online by designating a park of choice.

Tip for Hostels *... Purchase a simple key lock for locker storage. Bring your own personal items. Typical hostel charges vary from $15-25 per night, depending on choice of locale, bed, bunk or private room. Extra charges may apply for towels and blankets.*

Meals:

- For economical meals when driving, take along a cooler. Visit the local supermarket. Order a few slices of meat or cheese at the deli counter and roll them up for a snack. Fruit is another option. Farmers' markets are open early with fresh picked options. The huckleberries just outside Missoula were delicious!
- Miscellaneous Travel: I choose to drive, and so I keep my roadside emergency coverage current. However, travel by plane, bus, or train can be economical, informative and fun. All common carriers offer discounts for seniors. Go online to Amtrak for schedules and cost. Google "bus travel to" plus city of destination. Adapt travel to other than peak hours. Most volunteer organizations will pick you up at an airport or bus or train terminal if requested. For economical one-way trips, or information for renting an RV or driving a relocation car, check out the A-Z Grid in the back of this book.
- Thrift/Consignment Shops: Some of the best clothing can be found at consignment shops. Look for them in the phone book. I view thrift/consignments shops as just another way to recycle.
- Managing Personal Change: Goals change with age. We tend to allow past failures to predetermine future goals. Reminder: Expect what you want; don't expect what you don't want. Living in the past hampers our ability to focus on the future. Exercise mentally and physically since the loss of flexibility is directly related to the aging process. Retirement years should be the years of discovery with the advantage of experience. Age should not be a deterrent, but rather a stimulus to move on.

Tip for Travel .... *Check out discounted bus rates for seniors. Visit City Hall or the local Senior Center for transportation to shopping and health care. Retirement communities may provide rides to local destinations to residents.*

Change is perpetual. Change requires energy. With age, energy can become depleted by illness, circumstance, or depression, but it can be revitalized through social interaction, diet and exercise. I am motivated by thinking, "When I am eighty, do I want to wonder what if?" The answer for me is no.

Today I am focused and energized by looking forward to where I will be next and what I will do. Stagnation ages, mobility energizes. Cooperating mentally and physically with your environment will improve appearance and outlook. Security is an interior emotion. A home is an exterior structure. Truly, home is here the heart is.

The suggestions listed in this chapter are only a few of the options open to all who retire. To this end, I offer a new acronym: AAAA, Assess Assets (physical and psychological) and Adjust Accordingly. A personal assessment (see "Forms" in the back of this book) prior to retiring is invaluable while focusing on the years ahead. We are the curators of our contentment. Happiness is a learned behavior, and no one is too old to learn.

Tip for Living .... *Activate all five senses. Look at the scenery, hear the sound of the waterfall, smell the flowers, taste the chicken on the barbecue, and touch other lives in passing.*

Frequently Asked Questions

1. **How did you hear about the Golden Pass?** *When visiting Olympic National Park, the person in front of me had one. I asked and got one. This card may be obtained at the entrance of any national park at the booth. It is a wonderful cost saver!*

2. **What is a TripTik®?** *A TripTik is a booklet with step-by-step driving routes offered to AAA members. It is an excellent resource.*

3. **Any special travel advice?** *Toss a bag of cat litter into the trunk during winter travel. This material provides traction and can be used to absorb spills.*

Interview: Joan

Russian Orthodox Church, Kodiak Island, AK

Joan ... *teacher, mother, financial manager, bird enthusiast, and volunteer.*

In August, 2007, Joan sent the following e-mail: "I have arrived in Honduras and settled in! We number 20 in all at Our Little Roses Mission, of which the Holy Family Bilingual School is a component. About 25 'Little Roses' girls attend the school. The staff is well-qualified, mostly Honduran. I am the only volunteer who is bilingual. Our first responsibility was to revise the Vision and Mission statements, then begin teaching the new curriculum. A modern school has been built through contributions. Next door is the children's residence, courtyard style, with a fountain and garden in the center, and houses about 70 girls ranging from ages 3-18. The university-age girls live a few blocks away, in a residence next to ours, and we walk to and from school together."

Growing up in Ridgewood, New Jersey, Joan decided early on that she wanted to be in the Foreign Service. In seventh grade, she wrote a paper on Honduras and El Salvador, since her mother had been secretary to the El Salvadoran Consul in New York City. In ninth grade, while studying French, her class went to the United Nations where she witnessed simultaneous interpretation. She was hooked! Her sights were set on the Foreign Service.

"I always felt my life was spiraling into something purposeful," said Joan during one of our cell phone conversations between Arkansas and Honduras. "Looking back, it must have been a combination of my ambition and determination to be of service to the world, plus absolute faith that the outcome would be positive."

After graduation from Smith College in Northampton, Massachusetts, she took the Foreign Service exam and passed, but opted for a two-year deferment due to a fellowship to study Russian Language and History at Indiana University. "When I finish," she thought, "it will be the time for the foreign service." But it was 1966 and Joan was to be sidetracked by the Vietnam War.

"Since the ninth grade, I had dreamed of joining the foreign service," Joan sighed, "but because of the war, this option was gone. I told myself, someday."

A fellowship at Wesleyan University in Middletown, Connecticut, led to a Master's in teaching. The seventies came and went. She married, adopted two children—a Korean girl and a Filipino boy, placing her dreams of foreign service on hold. Joan became a full-time Mom and community volunteer.

Why Joan volunteers

"The school where I teach depends on volunteers to teach and care for their students. I was fortunate to have funded my retirement plan. I can afford to not be paid. I enjoy teaching these students English language skills enabling them to perhaps become leaders of their country, and teaching them to value their naturaleza and to become good world citizens. What could be more worthwhile and satisfying? This is probably the most important work I've ever done."

"Volunteering was and is a way of life for our family," Joan said. "We've collected items for the local clothing bank and raised money for causes—this was a passion! The children were involved, donating dollars to support a Filipino child and help homeless animals, and, while my daughter was at college, she was acknowledged for her volunteer efforts."

After a divorce in 1993, she met Mel, her lover/soul-mate/partner.

Together they traveled, combining Joan's love of language with adventure. But while touring The Galapagos Islands, Mel had a heart attack and died.

Distraught, Joan had to research how to return his body to the United States and learned that the gruesome task had to be arranged through the local consulate (see Chapter 7, Heed Needs for more information). While she was in the consulate waiting for some paperwork to be completed, she thought, "Now, is the time for foreign service."

However, then 9/11 happened. Once again, her dreams were put on hold. Besides, she thought, "...maybe I'm too old."

Honduras .... a land of birds, benevolence and Bougainvillea

Honduras is a democratic republic in Central America, granted independence by Spain in 1821. Most of the land is uninhabitable since the Sierra Madre range sweeps across it. Honduras boasts two coastlines. On the north is the Caribbean Sea and on the south, the Gulf of Fonesca.

About an hour's drive from the Caribbean coast, in the town of San Pedro Sula, is the Our Little Roses Ministry. San Pedro Sula has always played a major role in Honduran history. A Spanish conqueror founded it with the name of "Villa de San Pedro de Puerto Caballos" and within the next five years it became known as San Pedro Sula, with the name Sula deriving from the local dialect Usula, meaning "valley of birds."

Discouraged but not defeated, Joan heard about my retirement adventures and decided to apply to the Peace Corps. The process lumbered along until she was accepted, given a position and start date. "At last dreams are coming true!" she thought. But her elation was cut short. "After I told everyone about my plans, resigned my job, and rented my house," she e-mailed, "the Peace Corps called to say the position was no longer available. Can you believe that!?!" What to do?

After researching every volunteer site she could find, she was at church when her minister noticed her distress. "Have you heard about the Our Little Roses ministry?" he asked. Joan shook her head. Two weeks later, she had packed, updated her passport, and was set to go.

"People were surprised that I was going to do this, but I thought, why wait? Go now!" Joan's laugh traveled over the telephone lines from Honduras. "I had two catalysts, you and Mel."

It is a good feeling when determination and compassion meet at the crossroads. Through persistence, Joan did achieve her goal of Foreign Service. To keep those interested informed of her activities, she writes descriptive newsletters. The following excerpts are from those letters:

August:

The countryside is so beautiful! Flora and fauna, the incredible juxtaposition of the 16th and 17th centuries in San Pedro Sula, beautiful mountains, all cloud-shrouded at times, like a lady's shawl draped over a chair after a dance, glowing purple in the sunset. Courtyards are small, gated and locked, but lovely bougainvillea trees, hibiscus bushes, and topiary plants poke out between the bars into the street. Everyone is welcoming and friendly.

Honduras, and especially the Our Little Roses Ministry, sounds pretty nice, huh? Well, you don't get the picture until you look further into why the girls are here. Just beyond the school fence, which is topped by coils of barbed wire, is the "bordo," one of the shanty towns of San Pedro Sula. We're not allowed to cross over; two armed guards stand at the gate. This is where our girls came from, abandoned or abused, placed here by the judicial system. They appreciate the difference the home and school have made in their lives. After eighteen years, OLR has an excellent track record of success stories.

September:

I feel fortunate yet sad. Last night during a tropical storm, we devised ways of coping with the lack of electricity while enjoying our gas cook-stove, crank-up short-wave radio and full refrigerator, yet people in other parts of Honduras were losing their homes and drowning. The task is to help—you can't fix it, but you're not powerless.

The best part is the children. On the first day, I told them that I expected them to work hard "because they'd be the future leaders of Honduras some day and now is the time to prepare." They straightened and smiled, especially the girls who have had little opportunity to do much other than marry and take in laundry. School is easily disrupted, but I am up early to listen to the kiskidees sing on the electric wires. The birds-of-paradise and bougainvilleas line my walk to school, allowing quiet time to think about my time here and how I am going to make a difference.

October:

You should see how great these kids look in their school uniforms, freshly-scrubbed, shining like new pennies. My seventh grade class will be doing a recycling presentation for our Science Fair (Honduras does not seem to recycle). My rowdy eighth grade class is another story. Their project will be on alternative sources of fuel. We'll see.

The Spanish instruction here is outstanding! My competence is growing and I feel able to handle any situation. This is just what I hoped for.

November:

Guess what! We have a few dozen girls at various institutions of higher education. They must work to contribute to living expenses and maintain a certain GPA, but they do get a good education.

There is plenty to do! For all you wannabe volunteers or visitors from the U.S., we will be building and remodeling. Come on down!

When you come, you'll enjoy the atmosphere of Honduras: a tropical rain-forest park and a beautiful lake within a day-trip; Museums of Natural History and Anthropology; an interesting flea market with inexpensive treasures; delicious local dishes. I've been nosing around at every opportunity.

December:

Happy Holidays! I had a peak experience. Four adults and nine girls went on the school bus to purchase dresses and shoes for the holiday. Going to a mall is special. We had to teach two of the girls how to ride the escalator but managed to find smocked sundresses in pastel colors and black patent leather shoes. Christmas was different—no "O Come, O Come, Emmanuel," but, per Walter Cronkite, "That's the way it is."

35

2008:

I am depressed. This is the first time I've gone to the bordo, a place where people are really, really poor—houses made of random planks and pieces of wood, no running water or electricity. As mothers, it must hurt to know that their children will not have the chance for a better life. However, I see results. English language is essential. This is where I make a difference.

By the way, we live in a neighborhood here, just the way we did when I was growing up. I know my neighbors! There's Don Lucio and his grandchildren Diana, Marlon, Miyeli, Melanie; Milton, a kid with red hair who's always kicking a soccer ball. Lolly the parrot whistles at your back after you pass. There are hugs all around. Troubles are totally washed away by the time I arrive home. Home—what a nice word.

May:

It is a holiday! We are going to the beach. There's a fine mist on the mountains with dark outlines of the ridgelines, so the pearl-lustrous pastel colors of the sunrise will be muted. My two new parakeets chirp, answering others on the telephone wires. My birds were a surprise gift from a student—what a lovely gesture.

May Day was full of surprises. Because of the workers' demonstrations we could not get to the beach, so we went to the Zizima Water Park. In Honduras you become accustomed to interruptions. If you laugh and take it all in stride, it's even better!

The Saturday concert just started. There is a Neil Diamond song—"Beautiful Noise." Well, that's what it is like here. Early in the morning, dads go off on their motorbikes, then it's the kids splashing in blowup pools, little girls in panties, toddlers naked as newborns. I hear the trash collectors with their horse carts shouting, Llevo vos de la basura (I'll take your trash), the vegetable seller with his loudspeaker. Right about suppertime (the big meal is at noontime here) the lady who sells tortillas is singing. Since we have no doors to shut, we're right in the thick of things whether we like it or not, I like it fine!

2009: E-mail—Surprise news! I'm getting married to a wonderful Honduran man. We've known each other for two years. More to follow...

Joan's life has been an up and down spiral, but during our conversations about her adamant desire for serving abroad, how passionate she is about teaching and how overjoyed she is to be where she is, was apparent.

I will never forget the end of one call. "Retirement," she said with a sigh, "is one of the busiest times of my life, but doing what I want makes all the difference." Note: Joan is now married to a Honduran and resides in Honduras and the United States.

Joan's active participation in the five stages of retirement:
1. **Imagination**—*specializing in language study;*
2. **Anticipation**—*working toward her dream of foreign service;*
3. **Liberation**—*marriage, adoption, divorce and death, before dreams could be realized;*
4. **Transition**—*the Peace Corps application;*
5. **Reconciliation**—*fulfillment as a volunteer in a totally different and enchanting culture.*

THREE:

Choice and Voice

> *"If they give you ruled paper, write the other way."*
> -Juan Ramon Jimenez, poet,
> Nobel Prize, Literature (1881-1958)

Walking the rural Florida road to my volunteer assignment, the animal and bird symphony swells to a raucous cacophony as I enter the wildlife preserve. Peacocks strut with tail-feathers spread, prismatic emerald and sapphire hues illuminated by the tropical sun. Sleek Florida panthers pace and growl in their cages, anxious for breakfast. "Hello. Where's Sue?" squawks a white parrot, egotistically tossing his head. Polka-dotted guinea hens scurry under hibiscus trees laden with palm-sized lemony blooms. What an exotic place to be! After greeting the menagerie on a leisurely stroll around the diverse and exciting grounds of Arnold's Wildlife Rehabilitation and Butterfly Haven, I report for work.

Volunteering is an all-American tradition. Yet despite the large number of people who share their time and talents, the need remains overwhelming. Many of those who might like to volunteer have to remain in the workforce. Others are full-time caretakers, and some may feel they are already juggling too many responsibilities. Schedules are crammed, with no white space in the calendar left for time with family, much less philanthropy. Enter retirement, a time of release from daily structure, offering flexible hours to devote to an array of activities.

Some 45 million Americans participate in volunteer activities and about one-third of them are seniors.[2] I prefer the name "mature adult"! Thirty-six

---

2   AARP Magazine, Nov/Dec 2006, Leap Into a New Career, article by Samuel Green

million Americans are now 65 and older, officially labeled senior. These mature adult are generally healthier and more active than their predecessors. Their basic reason for retirement is "to do other things," but, even if the choice is to retire early, say at age fifty-five, now is the time to venture outside the box. Think of retirement as a catalog of options, each representing a variety of styles, sizes, and shapes awaiting perusal. A volunteer retirement lifestyle is one of those options.

Think can vs. should. What can I do rather than what should I do? Should I continue to follow the same routine? Should I meet with the same people? Should I serve on the same committees? Some may answer yes. But for those investigating options, live those questions now.

What Can I Do?

- *Specify your objectives.*
- *Create alternatives.*
- *Understand the consequences.*
- *Clarify the uncertainties.*

OR consider... .

What Else Can I Try?

- *Develop a hobby into a marketable skill.*
- *Learn or renew a skill by returning to school.*
- *Start an Internet business.*
- *Update skills to fit current needs.*

Volunteer positions come in all sizes and shapes—part-time, full-time, sporadic or scheduled. If you are not available to volunteer on a regular basis at home or away, try researching opportunities to volunteer on call.

If it is difficult for you to get around, assist in fund-raising, write an article for the paper, or serve on a telephone calling tree. All of these "virtual volunteering" activities may be accomplished from the comfort of home. Share your expertise with those in long-term nursing facilities. Read to preschoolers. Donate time at the local animal shelter. Help with a special project at a local assisted-living facility, such as setting up a butterfly garden, or leading a sing-a-long, exercise, or arts and crafts class.

All those hours previously filled with working are now available, inviting your participation. "But, wait," you say, "not right now. I can't afford to take off for new horizons and new adventures. That takes money and I am not a millionaire, not even a thousandaire!" Yet a bit of planning may allow you to stretch those limited dollars much farther than you imagine.

Put voice and action to choice. Investigate options, research new places, adapt current skills to a creative project, or begin a new activity. While doing so, you will notice your circle of friends increase.

Many readers will remember the time when a child was born into a line of work. A teacher's child became a teacher, doctor's son a doctor, a plumber's son a plumber. Now there is choice. In the 1950's most college-age women became a nurse or a teacher, or got married.

When I was growing up, I had hoped to do something in the arts, but had not yet found my voice so instead settled for marriage. In my world of volunteering, I inject creativity whenever possible. If you have a suppressed talent anxious to surface, bring it forth now! The future is here. Draw on hidden or unrecognized skills to pattern the remainder of your life.

Whenever possible, avoid the monotonous grind of repetition. It can become a habit.

Not too long ago I read...
Thoughts become words,
Words become actions,
Actions become habits,
Habits become character,
Character becomes destiny.
-Anonymous

Although life is moving at warp speed, create a destiny worthy of your character and skills. Perhaps daily life is a habit, a predictable routine. It works in education and the military, but not retirement. This is a time of discovery!

Eliminate the drudgery by revitalizing your objectives. Exchange the routine for adventures, even small ones. Allow positive attitudes to ripple out. Enthusiasm is contagious. It might even cause others to explore—to delve into the volunteer world.

Updating current ideals and perceptions does not mean discarding old values. Forget about what used to be. Think of a new goal, picture that it might be fun, and try it. Simply put one foot in front of the other.

The ultimate goal of retirement is satisfaction. Discuss options and alternatives with family, friends, and advisors, knowing that the ultimate decision rests with only one person, you.

Choice is like an iceberg. There is a lot hidden under the surface. Choice is the ultimate in self-determination but guard against overload. Do not create an option merry-go-round. Make lists, discuss, eliminate, revise, discuss, strategize, and revise.

Adventures come from all directions. I was able to visit the Everglades, canoe the Loxahatchee Wildlife Refuge, re-visit the history of the Seminole Indians and Trail of Tears, and walk the beach on the Gold Coast.

Beef cattle, Sand Hill Cranes and Butterflies ....

My second opportunity to volunteer came through friends I met while working at Vassar College in Poughkeepsie, New York. In the 1980's Betty and Al retired to Lake Okeechobee, Florida. "If you're going to volunteer all over the place," they asked, "why not volunteer down here and stay with us." They are gracious hospitable people and offered me a private room and bath. I am fortunate to know them and their affable dog Daisy. 'Down here' turned out to be Arnold's Wildlife Rehabilitation and Butterfly Haven (see A-Z grid for site address) in Okeechobee. Sue Arnold, owner and master naturalist, was looking for someone to obtain a grant to produce a DVD describing the life cycle of the butterfly in the Okeechobee area for presentation to school children grades K-5. Along with my administrative assistant responsibilities, I weeded and pruned a garden designed to resemble the colorful striped Zebra, Florida's State butterfly, guidance provided by expert hands. On a recent visit, Sue said, "Come see our newest residents." In the clinic area were two marmosets frolicking in a cage, sipping nectar. "These two were found in a duffle bag at the end of the driveway this morning, unwanted, discarded. It's unfair." Since I was volunteering from January through April, occasionally there were frost warnings. As soon as a warning was issued, all volunteers and

41

staff scurried to cover indigenous butterfly-friendly plants with blankets, sheets, and quilts. The next morning we re-assembled to help fold and store. A great opportunity to socialize. Although I was unaware what my contribution would be prior to arriving in Florida, responsibilities were discussed and time spent was enjoyable and beneficial to all.

Positives and Negatives:

As in the workplace, viewpoint is not always harmonious among volunteers. A volunteer position, even though it may not be a nine-to-five routine, does possess some of the same qualities as a paid position. The expectation is that a volunteer will report for work on time and fulfill all responsibilities assigned by the volunteer coordinator.

Long-term, long-distance volunteering is a non-traditional form of volunteering. In local, short-term volunteering, mature adult may set their own schedule and interrupt it for any reason they choose. Accepting room and board as payment brings the additional responsibility of a forty-hour work week. If a shorter schedule is desired, speak with the volunteer coordinator prior to accepting an assignment.

Sound familiar? Not much different from the workplace. First-time volunteers can practice a little prevention by thinking back to a rule they learned in kindergarten: STOP, LOOK, and LISTEN. Observe before speaking. This prevents foot-in-mouth syndrome. It is always better to err on the side of silence when you are in a strange environment. You might be an expert at a certain task, but performing it as a volunteer may require a certain amount of diplomacy. On the first day of a new assignment, step back, look around, and assess the situation. Save your suggestions for later, perhaps.

All volunteers must realize that this is not the old workplace. Control is not appropriate in this new environment. Let go. Self-confidence can be your best friend or your worst enemy. It's not about what is done or said, it's about how it is done or said. It's also about wanting to serve, rather than having to report for work.

As a supervisor, every volunteer director must coordinate multigenerational personalities to achieve positive results. They are there to listen and solve problems. If there is a family emergency or an illness or a circumstance that requires a change in your responsibilities or length of service, speak with those in charge. Give someone in authority a chance to effect resolution of a given situation. Utilize choice and voice.

Types of Volunteers:

1. Martyr: There are two kinds: those who work day and night without whining because it's what they wish to do, and those who work day and night, whining continually about how exhausted they are, expecting sympathy and gratitude.

2. Martyr-Egghead: A prince or princess with a smug expression. Their way is the only way because they have been volunteering at the same place forever and know all there is to know.

3. Most-of-us: Those who do the job, share skills, enjoy the experience, and leave at the appropriate time.

Volunteers in long-term, long-distance assignments interact with multigenerational, multi-skilled individuals, performing tasks from the menial to the essential. Common concerns relating to family may be voiced or shared, or not. The amount of personal involvement with other volunteers is up to the individual. The predominant concern is service and compassion.

Keep in mind that accepting a long-term (anything over 30 days) volunteer assignment with room and board means that the assignment becomes a job with all the ramifications thereof. The position is not a vacation. There will be time for recreation on earned days off. If time is required or desired for additional travel, ask permission from a supervisor. It may or may not be possible. Clarify. When volunteering, follow a good work ethic, but remember that work ethics differ within a multigenerational environment.

Discrepancies to Discuss:

1. Schedule: Schedule assignments differ. For example at the college in Alaska, some volunteers were on an academic schedule and others a year-round schedule although both received the same benefits.

Solution: At the holiday break, I discussed the situation with my immediate supervisor who recognized the inequity. We resolved the issue within the office and although this was not something I could have anticipated, it was a lesson learned about issues to clarify before taking my next assignment. Clarify your schedule in relation to other positions offered prior to reporting for an assignment.

2. Housing: Volunteer housing is usually adequate and comfortable, but not luxurious. Rooms are often furnished with dated furniture and there is little or no storage. A volunteer may be housed in a dorm, with or without a roommate. With the shared housing in Alaska, it was a pleasure to work and interact with six very talented women. We were flexible, able to compromise and prioritize. Each room was private, although bathrooms were shared.

Solution: Prior to accepting a volunteer position, make a point to discuss housing, especially if privacy is an issue.

3. Responsibilities: Clarify. Clarify. Clarify. Although I asked many questions about what, why, when, and where, I did not ask all the right questions. My responsibilities in Sitka proved to be far more demanding than anticipated. Upon arrival I learned that due to circumstances my responsibilities had changed. I had a choice—stay or go. If you feel the job presented is more than expected, you do have the right to ask for another assignment. Every volunteer experience is an opportunity to assist and learn.

Solution: If an unanticipated situation occurs, discuss it with your supervisor or the volunteer coordinator. When volunteering, the first rule is find your voice to express compassion and share skills. Do not dive in before making sure there is water in the pool. Write questions down prior to speaking on the phone, so when the volunteer director asks for background to match skills with the position offered, you will be able to answer. (See the Evaluation Form at the end of this book for help in this area.)

E-mail communication is great for documentation. Really think about commitment and adventure. When asked to send a resume, remember it is your choice to share or not. If your choice is to volunteer at a position totally different from your workplace, it may be prudent to describe some skills, keeping others to yourself.

4. Socializing: Adventures come to fruition through curiosity. To make the most of a new volunteer destination, read the local papers for events at a local library or volunteer site. Most events I attended were either free or offered at a nominal fee. Go, enjoy, learn and, meet new friends.

Volunteers in volunteer housing participate in games, meetings and special events, such as pot-luck suppers, yoga, and trips to town or local sightseeing. A car is an asset. I offered rides when going to the library or to town. This was a courtesy on my part, never an expectation.

Each day of volunteering is a new opportunity to learn. Where else but in the volunteer world would a job offer free housing and meals? Where else is there an opportunity to mingle with butterflies, or milk goats while explaining how to reduce world hunger to visitors?

Most volunteers, if they research appropriately, will find their niche. When online, type in "volunteer" and watch what pops up. Internet information is continually updated. When in doubt, just browse. Remember, it is up to the individual volunteer to specify skills, schedule, and location.

There may come a time when a decision to volunteer is questioned by family, friends, or co-workers. Try not to let others dissuade you. Prepare a defense for opposition. I did not anticipate negativity from those around me since I thoroughly researched options was ready to answer questions with enthusiasm. Utilize choice and voice.

Reinforce the positive. Explore alternatives and possibilities. Do not dwell on the outcome. Life has a way of accelerating as we age. Those with imagination not only look for possibilities, they make them happen. As a friend's newsletter states, "We must be willing to take charge of our own future, which may require making things up as we go along."

Questions to Ask:
- *Why am I interested in volunteering?*
- *What type of activities do I enjoy?*
- *Can I commit to what the organization is requesting in time and talent?*
Write responses to these questions PRIOR to calling or e-mailing regarding any opportunity:

The following are a few of the more popular volunteer opportunities, along with my comments from personal experience. Others are listed on the categorized A-Z table the back of this book:

- AARP www.aarp.com

AARP offers a range of opportunities where volunteers can put their time, skills and experience to good use. Although I haven't volunteered directly with AARP, I utilize the site as a resource on retirement issues. If a member, register with their Volunteer Talent Bank.

- AmeriCorps VISTA www.vista.gov

This agency, a division of the Peace Corps, administers domestic volunteer programs. The agency will direct volunteers to projects within their own community. Student volunteers at Heifer were serving with this program and their enthusiasm was apparent.

- Habitat For Humanity www.habitatforhumanity.org

Habitat is a nonprofit, ecumenical Christian housing ministry that seeks to eliminate poverty and homelessness from the world, and to make decent shelter a matter of conscience and action. Habitat for Humanity invites people of all backgrounds, races and religions to build houses in partnership with families in need. Perhaps one day I will connect with a project.

- Heifer International www.heifer.org

Heifer is all about new beginnings. It is devoted to helping impoverished families, in the United States and around the globe, become self-reliant. Its mission is to work with communities to end hunger and poverty in the world by sharing animal offspring, along with knowledge, resources, and skills in an expanding network of hope, dignity, and self-reliance. Heifer envisions a world of communities living together in peace, equitably sharing the resources of a healthy planet. It is a community development organization rather than a relief organization such as the Red Cross. To that end, it partners with community groups that form specific goals to achieve a self-sustaining environment. Heifer provides expertise in animal health, water quality, gender equity, the environment, and community development. Their educational mission is to help people understand the root causes of world hunger. Take a look at their site.

Greeting visitors and feeding goats .... *My third volunteer experience was at the Heifer Ranch in Perryville, Arkansas, an affiliate of Heifer International, a nonprofit organization dedicated to relieving global hunger and poverty. Their administrative headquarters are located in Little Rock. Again,* through word-of-mouth, I learned of the learning center which offered many volunteer opportunities. Well, I had never been to Arkansas, so... The Heifer Ranch Learning Center in Perryville is a 1,200-acre working farm that includes a 200-acre learning center. It welcomes multigenerational volunteers to work with livestock, organic gardening, maintenance, education and administration. I arrived in February, and coming from the Northeast, I expected warmth—wrong! I was surprised to find the temperature in the 30s. An inch of snow appeared and disappeared quickly, but then 2008 had a lot of peculiar weather, world-wide. Since I drove, I was able to bring along clothing for summer and winter, but I didn't bring enough corduroys. Thank goodness there was a washer and dryer. I was assigned to Administration, as receptionist for the ranch. At first, I performed my duties in the Accounting Office. Then was placed in the Visitor Center to help greet visitors while still acting as receptionist and assisting as needed. This was great! Housing at the ranch was a two-bedroom home shared with Sue and Ken, an energetic couple from Michigan who brought along dominos, and we had some excellent games. They worked with livestock, long, hard hours, but it was what they wanted to do. It not only provided them with responsibilities that were totally removed from their educational backgrounds, but also gave them respite from the snowy Upper Peninsula of Michigan. While at Heifer, I gathered fresh chicken and duck eggs from the barn for breakfast and to make custard, milked and fed baby goats, hiked Petit Jean Mountain and the Buffalo River area, visited Tahlequah, Oklahoma, home of the Cherokee Nation, and drove to Hot Springs where rejuvenating waters flow. I thoroughly enjoyed my experience and hope to return. My time with Heifer inspired and empowered me to spread their positive message. Contact the Director of Volunteers at Heifer for opportunities.

- Nomads www.nomads.com

This is a term for individuals in RVs who share their expertise by volunteering. They accomplish projects through many organizations, including the National Park Service. Some call themselves "turtles" since they travel with their home on their back. They do not need room and board; simply hook up in exchange for their services. This is yet another option to consider if you are willing to purchase an RV and absorb the expense of gas and insurance. Nomads are very enthusiastic about sharing their experiences. There are numerous communities of people who choose to live and or travel without the financial drain of a permanent dwelling. (See Chapter 4)

- Peace Corps www.peacecorps.gov

This popular government agency administers projects in more than 70 countries. Peace Corps volunteers arrive at an assigned destination, not with funds or equipment, but with willingness to adapt their skills and knowledge to the community. If you are seeking a long-term assignment with foreign travel, the Peace Corps may be a good match for you. As with most government agencies, there are qualifications, objectives, restrictions, and exit benefits. From personal experience, I will say the application process is cumbersome and frustrating. The site advocates patience. Communication with my liaison was tedious. Eventually, my decision to withdraw my application was primarily based on the required length of service, 26 months. I did not want to be away from my family for that long. If you are concerned about safety, peruse news services such as www.bbc.org for the current status of your assigned location. I was told that the Federal government does covet the services of the 50+ crowd and hopes their numbers will increase because age and experience are respected in the Third World.

- Presbyterian Church http://www.pcusa.org

PCUSA offers volunteer opportunities in ministries that include camps and conference centers, governing bodies, nonprofit agencies, congregational life, child and adolescent care, health care, refugee services, elderly services, higher education, and social welfare. Most of the volunteers I worked with in Alaska came via PCUSA. Many are now friends. PCUSA offers opportunities in the United States and abroad.

- United Church of Christ http://www.ucc.org

UCC asks the question: what can I do with my life? How can I make a difference? One way is through Volunteer Ministries partnering with local agencies to place individual volunteers, matching their skills with the needs of a community. My volunteering with UCC was in River Ridge, Louisiana, rehabbing a house damaged by Hurricane Katrina with a well-qualified group from Wisconsin that was on its third trip to Louisiana. I simply followed their lead. The church asks that at least some of the group be knowledgeable in home repair to serve as crew leaders. The Disaster

Recovery Office identifies work projects, schedules volunteer groups, and coordinates efforts in the New Orleans area.

In the world of volunteering, many types of expertise are needed and anything goes! Adult literacy groups are always looking for volunteers. Volunteer payment is a combination of camaraderie and self-esteem, plus the opportunity to stay active and involved and continually enrich the lives of all involved.

There is no time like the present to begin the rest of our lives. As birthdays accumulate, act on your dreams before they slip through the cracks. Illness, financial setbacks and family issues all interrupt. Volunteer coordinators will make time to sit down and discuss issues. There is always the opportunity to return.

Relax and float with the current. It is time to stop swimming upstream. As a volunteer, interaction is within a multigenerational environment. Being with the younger generation keeps everyone young! In our daily lives, between competition and accountability, our pace seems to accelerate.

Try not to be a frantic enabler, attempting to fix or solve. If anxiety or overwork should surface, give yourself some time to do nothing. Find someplace to retreat in complete privacy. Allow time to ponder. Then, speak calmly and confidently with those who can help. Pay attention. Listen to feedback.

Remember, age is relevant and important only with wine or the date on yogurt. My mother was old at twenty. My grandmother never seemed to reach the point at which others shut themselves off from stimulation or participation. Observe how young eyes bubble with vitality, like champagne. Older eyes can sometimes be tainted from the dregs of the barrel. Let age be the luxury of memory combined with the wisdom of the past plus the courage to wonder about tomorrow.

Take the opportunity to share stories. Make memories. Share memories. Embrace life. Volunteering combines the best of this, enabling choice and voice to all.

Frequently Asked Questions

1. *How do I find these opportunities? Go online and search. Enter the word "volunteer" into the search bar along with a desired location. Peruse the resources*

listed at the back of this book. Speak with other volunteers and listen to their experiences.

2. **How can I be sure an organization is legitimate?** *The best defense is research, research, research. Before I decided to adopt this particular retirement lifestyle, I spent hours at the computer. Before making a commitment, ask for names of current or past volunteers. Follow through, and contact each for their opinion.*

3. **What about volunteer vacations?** *A volunteer vacation is a specific activity for a specific length of time in a specific area where vacationing volunteers may, at a cost, assist in a project while residing in various types of housing. Google Elderhostel or Global Volunteers. All offer a number of long-and short-term volunteer vacations in the U.S. or abroad for a fee. Check out the Grid at the back of this book.*

Interview: Ken and Sue

Heifer Learning Center, Perryville, AR

Ken ... *educator, father, woodcrafter, sea captain, fisherman extraordinaire, and volunteer.*

Sue ... *educator, mother, EMT, avid reader, grant writer, domino enthusiast and volunteer.*

Ken and Sue are Yoopers, an affectionate term for residents of the Upper Peninsula of Michigan, and live so far north their two sons have dual citizenship with Canada. Sue says with a laugh, "The hospital in Sault Ste. Marie, Ontario was an hours' drive, but had an excellent neonatal unit. Dual citizenship came with the delivery!"

In February, when the snow is high and the temperature low, they pack their car and head south. One might think they would drive to some sunny beach, but their destination is the Heifer Learning Center Ranch in Perryville, Arkansas where they gather eggs, walk goats and birth calves. Forty hours a week of manual labor, and they love it!

Both Ken and Sue were teachers. Sue was in Special Education for ten years before becoming an elementary school reading coordinator. Along with being the K-12 art teacher, she taught grades 4-6; then moved on to middle-school English, Social Studies and Reproductive Health. Her experience with varied age groups and cultures helped later in travel and volunteering.

Why Sue volunteers..... *"Because we can. Because we should. Besides, we combine fun stuff and work stuff a lot of the time and the work stuff becomes just as much fun as the fun stuff!"*

"I really never reached the point of burn-out! How many people do you know that loved their job for thirty years?"

Ken enjoyed teaching music and math for a few years before moving to administration. After receiving a master's degree in Counseling he worked within a multi-county school organization which provided services too costly for local schools. Quickly climbing the administrative ladder, Ken was soon overseeing state and federal programs, stimulating work with frequent travel to Lansing, the State Capital. Eventually, to spend more time with his growing family, Ken accepted a position as local School Superintendent.

Why Ken volunteers.... *"I feel we have been extraordinarily blessed and this is my way of paying forward along with expressing gratitude."*

Seated comfortably on the couch at Gate House on the Heifer Ranch in Arkansas, Sue reflected on the issue of family culture, stating that volunteering is not a new concept in their family. At home, Sue served on the Library Board, as Secretary for the Ambulance Corps, and in numerous other capacities writing grants, enlisting and training volunteers while being a volunteer herself.

When approached about the need for emergency medical technicians, she took the training and now serves with the Ambulance Corps. "The children were old enough to be without me if I had to leave in the middle of the night," she said, "though I will admit the course was challenging!"

The couple feels they are fortunate to have spent their entire lives in the same town, even the same house, raising their two sons among family and friends.

There's a pig in the cistern!

"At Heifer, resourcefulness, one trait that develops with age—is the name of the game." Ken smiled as he recalled the day a pig fell into the cistern.

One afternoon, the pigs escaped their pen and were running in and around an adjacent pasture. When rounding them up, someone heard a squeal and looked down to see that one had fallen into the cistern, a large hole designed to hold water. The pig weighed about one-hundred pounds and was at least five feet down.

"When I think back, I laugh," Ken said, "but you have to realize this really is serious. If a pig gets overworked, it can have a heart attack and die. We had to figure out how to get him out of there, quick."

As is the case with many non-profit organizations, Heifer depends on donations to purchase supplies, so no crane or lifting device other than a backhoe was available and that was down by the maintenance building. Ken quickly assessed the situation. Horse halters were brought from the barn to fasten around the front and hind quarters, so that the pig would be able to breathe and not choke while being hoisted. With the help of many hands, this very large parcel of pork was in one swoop lifted up and out and released to scoot happily across the pasture.

"Few people would understand our elation at the pig running free!" Ken said. "Granted, he had to be herded back into the pen but... that's another story."

"Way back when," Ken said, "I bought a bare-bones cabin on the North Shore of Lake Huron that we've enlarged, renovated and rearranged. We now have a beautiful home convenient to fishing and all sorts of recreational activities." After he retired, an acquaintance called Ken to ask, "Ever entertain the idea of a charter fishing boat?" Ken found himself back in the classroom obtaining a Great Lakes Sea Captain's License, and now caters to the summer fishing crowd along with piloting local cruises on Lake Huron.

These skills only scratch the surface of this multi-talented couple, who are evenly matched in their enthusiasm for volunteering. One year, after their son raised money for Heifer, they decided Christmas would involve Heifer instead of glitter and glitz. Some family members seemed surprised (but too polite to comment). To those who did, Sue and Ken explained the impact of such a worthwhile program. Later, when considering retirement options, they Googled volunteer opportunities and Heifer popped up.

When making their commitment to Heifer the discussion centered on education vs. opportunity: to do something new. Both were in total agreement in choosing livestock since Sue's grandfather was a dairy farmer, and Ken grew up on a farm. "I had my share of chasing cows!" he recalled.

Aware of the hard manual labor assigned to livestock volunteers, for their first long-distance volunteer effort, Sue and Ken committed to only six weeks, feeling it would serve as a prudent experiment—if they could hold up to the demands. If? Of course; they stayed six weeks plus.

"Oh, it's not all cute little bunnies and sweet smelling hay," Sue said, pointing to her soiled shirt hanging in the kitchen. "There is slop and manure and all sorts of unglamorous tasks, but since this is our fourth time, knowledge of the routine makes it easier for all. Some days are just plain drudgery, but that's life. Like I said before, the fun stuff and the work stuff meld."

Up to the point of retirement, Ken had questioned his colleagues about timing. How would he know it was time to retire? They said, "You'll know." Ken laughed. "They were right. One day I realized I was ready for something new."

Some options included renovating his neglected hunting camp and being asked to evaluate the possibility of building an assisted living facility in his community. A fortuitous trip down-state to visit an ailing aunt led to the discovery that a family member owned a few assisted living facilities. Good timing! Within two years, the project was completed.

At Heifer, Ken's woodworking and renovation skills are utilized along with ideas for making the workday easier. Sue is appreciative of her EMT instruction and experiences since they have been invaluable dealing with birthing sheep, goats and cows, recalling, "anytime there is a life-or-death situation, there is bonding. Last year we stayed up all night with a new baby lamb. It's hard to walk away when a newborn might not survive."

Among his varied talents, Ken is an excellent photographer. He has accumulated numerous shots from necropsies for livestock documentation to the exciting landscapes of Australia, providing many digital memories to peruse, along with bumps and bruises from birthing sheep, building fences, and mucking stalls. They both agree that every day has its challenges.

"But," Sue said, slowly straightening her back after a day of painting shield boards for the newest pasture, "I want to wear out, not rust out!"

Ken and Sue's active participation in the four (reduced from five) stages of retirement:

1. **Imagination**—*"It didn't take much imagination,"* Sue said. *"It was simply a continuation of our lifestyle. We knew we would be busy doing something and considered it fortunate that we had lived modestly within our means while working, providing the financial resources necessary to fund the freedom to enjoy our retirement."*

2. **Anticipation and Liberation combined**—*Ken and Sue discussed choices in retirement. The wow-we-don't-have-to-getup-this-morning feeling faded quickly. Since both had enjoyed their educational careers, retirement was a bit wistful, but without regrets, simply a bit of melancholy combined with the anticipation of change.*

3. **Transition**—*They were willing participants in a combination of travel and volunteering.*

4. **Reconciliation**—*They realized their lifestyle is an excellent melding of hopes and dreams for travel while learning more about the world, as well as staunch commitment to service.*

FOUR:
Scheme to Team...or Not

Think before you speak
one can't extract an arrow
without damage.

Dave Nylan, Haiku poet

What do Oprah Winfrey and Spiderman have in common? Take a guess. Correct—they're both single.

Of the estimated 93 million single adults in the United States, more than one third are fifty or older, living alone voluntarily or involuntarily, due to choice or circumstance. Singleness today is not only tolerated, it is embraced. To most, being single suggests freedom, independence, and opportunities to better oneself without guilt.

There are no rules to being single. Singleness is a lifestyle in transition, a mode that most are not prepared to accept until circumstances present. Those who are or will become single, slide into the status like Cinderella into her slipper. Singleness is life with self-responsibility. It is spontaneity personified. Being single does not necessarily mean being alone, nor does it mean being lonely. We will probably never become a nation of singles, but there's a certain smugness associated with not having to share the remote.

Some single retirees covet quiet space without interruption; others prefer social interaction accompanied by noise and disruption. Singles choose surroundings that meet their emotional and financial needs. If, after a while, those needs change, a single is more likely to begin the search for a new environment. Financial resources do determine lifestyle. A beautiful and simple one is available to everyone. It's all about need vs. want.

Experiencing local culture in Alaska .... One day I heard that you could learn how to make authentic Tlingit moccasins at the Totem National Park, so a housemate and I went to investigate.

Margaret, a native Alaskan of the Tlingit tribe, who learned the art of beading from her mother and grandmother, greeted us. "There is a prerequisite," she said. "You must first complete three beading projects"; emphasizing the focus needed in the meticulous beading and sewing process.

Also, if you work with sealskin you must be under the direction of a native Alaskan. Margaret is Tlingit, knowledgeable and creative, full of stories about Sitka and tribal traditions—a pleasure to be around.

While stitching the sole to the instep with sinew, Margaret explained why older Alaskan women appear to be missing their front teeth. "When you slip your foot into a new moccasin," she said, "your toes rub against the ridge of stitching. Alaskan women chewed these bulky edges until soft, reducing their teeth to nubs."

For us, she offered a ball peen hammer. My moccasins, beaded in a spring-summer-fall-winter Tlingit leaf pattern are a treasure.

According to recent research, one in three baby boomers can expect an aging parent to move in with them within the next five to ten years. This arrangement can be as separate or as integrated as desired.

Sharing a home offers independence to aging parents, while allowing children to oversee daily care. Renovations may cause hesitation however it is not a risky investment since the space can always be converted back into a home office or living space for an adult child. A friend who renovated space for her parents said, "The economy and peace of mind of being together simply makes sense. It was the right thing to do for our family."

Remember all those old movies where houses were multi-generational? Three families under the same roof were commonplace, elderly on the first floor, family with children on the second, singles on the third. While many seniors are not ready, or willing, to provide essential services to their children or be on call, a multi-generational home may be a convenient solution.

If housing presents financial problems, try stretching your budget by sharing space. Advertise for a roommate; arrange for expenses to be divided. A more radical approach would be to purchase a dwelling and share expenses as a group. This option requires legal research and may demand a good deal of discussion regarding budget and privacy issues, but do not discount it before investigation if it seems logical for your situation.

Many retirees who thought they could not imagine ever leaving the family homestead are able do so without major heartbreak. Perhaps a child would wish to occupy the family home? What about a roommate (though keep in mind that it may not be like the Golden Girls)? Perhaps selling and making an entire new beginning would be the best option. Focus on your most desirable outcome.

Fixed housing costs can be like a leaky faucet, drip, drip, dripping away precious dollars. If, as a single or a couple, it is possible to stay in your home, great; if not, reduce your financial and environmental footprint before you are forced to, before your present housing becomes a fiscal albatross. Go through all the "perhaps" scenarios and ask yourself, "What if a flood or a hurricane was coming and we had to leave RIGHT NOW! What would we take?"

It is liberating to realize how much can be left behind. It is also fun to clean out drawers, attics and storage places, looking through pictures and papers, deciding which is important enough to keep.

Unforeseen cause and effect: *Boomers will be the first generation in history to bypass the chore of growing old. With scientific breakthroughs in aging, future generations will most likely burn-out rather than physically deteriorate. Older Americans can look forward to more retirement years, more careers, more relocation, and more options.*

Dispose of possessions by recycling, donating, or simply passing on-down. It is my personal opinion that recycling is an ongoing volunteer opportunity, which can be accomplished at home or away, as a single or as a group. Remember the three R's: Reuse, Reduce, Recycle. Practicing the first two should eliminate the third. Go to www.recycle.com or www.earth911.org for more information.

Downsizing is daunting, but not impossible. Ask for help. Tossing or allocating is much easier when another person is present to help in decision-making. Sell on-line or offer local shelters items which can be used by those attempting to furnish a new home. Call household friendly organizations to pick-up larger reusable items.

The group most at-risk in retirement is single women. Almost three-quarters of the elderly population are single women who hover around the poverty level. Women who assume traditional care-giving roles accrue less retirement income in a system that bases its calculation on earnings and time spent on the job. This also means less Social Security income as well. Further, women are often paid less than their male counterparts, and some work part-time which further decreases the accumulation of Social Security credits.

Also, be aware of the other side of being a single. Yes, you have the freedom and independence to be responsible for yourself, to go where you want, when you want, but I would be remiss if I didn't mention the issue of being a single among couples. When you're married or with a partner, the tendency is to think in the number two; you are with someone and assume everyone else is also. Not so.

Cause and effect .... *After I sold my condo, I was homeless for almost two years. In Alaska, I had an entire year free of taxes and maintenance to consider my options. One consequence of purchasing a home is an automatic extension of roots and responsibility. Accumulated social connections may complicate a change of lifestyle. The purchase of a smaller home may provide a stable environment, a place to return to, and a place to store belongings. A sense of place may not be important when you are thirty-something, but takes on a different meaning entirely as retirement approaches. However, a sense of place does not need to be a permanent dwelling. Truly, home is where the heart is.*

In volunteer communities, people tend to separate into two groups—under thirty and over thirty, though all ages do interact, and there are some who move in both groups. However there are times when older singles are excluded simply by oversight.

When I was in Alaska, there were seven single women housed in close proximity in a communal setting so that exclusion was not an issue. This is not always the case. As a single, you could find yourself the only one in the group. If this happens, make an effort to talk about your interests. Check out what is going on when and where. Speak up and ask to be included. This could make the problem disappear. If not, inquire as to the ratio of single to married before agreeing to the next assignment.

Regarding couples, keep in mind that if one spouse should live beyond the other's pension allotment, and the pension does not provide income dollars after the primary beneficiary's death, the surviving spouse must survive on Social Security income alone. When discussing retirement as a couple, think about who will be left with what and if that amount will be enough to live on comfortably.

Explore the possibility of leaving a partial benefit behind for the "surviving spouse." Granted, the immediate pension amount will be lessened and there is a risk that the anticipated may never occur, but sometimes life takes strange turns. Bear in mind that the surviving spouse will be single with the expectation of living, not simply existing.

It is obvious that the ratio of older single women to older single men is disproportionate. In some social situations this may cause anxiety and isolation. Although many gender issues no longer exist, there are still "unacceptable" situations for women. Keep this in mind when volunteering at remote locations.

Most likely a woman will find herself with less disposable income than a man. To compound this, women think of power differently from men. They tend to define it as the ability to maintain control over their own lives. Instead of needing to dominate, they may be more inclined to use guilt or behind-the-scenes manipulation. Some of us grew up in the presence of mothers without power. Consequently we turn to networking to reach out. According to Gloria Steinem in her book, *Outrageous Acts and Everyday Rebellions,* "Networks are psychic territory and every woman needs a free place, a little psychic territory."

Further, single men and women require different strategies for retirement than married couples. Some couples may survive on a shoestring by playing off each others strengths. Singles may need a miracle to survive. Retirement volunteering with organizations that offer room and board might just be that miracle.

Now let's talk about single men. In the January 2008, AARP Bulletin, Julia M. Klein, cultural reporter and critic, writes, "Men have their issues also. Married men are paid more than single men; the assumption being that a married person has to earn enough to provide for a spouse.... Men tell me they can be happy as singles. Some men will say they've learned to use the microwave, do the laundry and make their own bed. However, older single men do confide that they feel more 'comfortable' participating in social opportunities as a couple."

Social issues include how women covet friendships; men differ in that arena as well. They may have football friends or hunting buddies, but these are different from the call-in-the-middle-of-the-night friendships that women enjoy. The other issue is control or power. As mentioned earlier, women define power differently than men. Men tend to define power as dominance, a trait single women view as intolerable.

Housing Options:
- **Team-up**—share a home with a partner or roommate. Place an ad on a local bulletin board or post a notice at the Senior Center. The response may be more than you expect. For women, look for a "Crone's Nest" in the area. This is a house shared by two or three women, usually older, but not necessarily so, who share housework and pool resources, attempting to stretch dollars. Get A Foxy Old Woman's Guide to Living with Friends (Crossing Press) from the local library. Inquire about housing options at the Senior Center or local library.
- **Share a home with family**. When my son purchased a home and offered in-law space, I wanted to accept, but since two grandchildren were involved, I was hesitant about becoming a nanny rather than Nana. However, this home base allows the freedom to come and go as my volunteer retirement lifestyle requires. When I take on an assignment, I simply walk out and shut the door. It is the perfect solution for our family. Separate entrances encourage privacy and communication. Do not assume, and above all, do not take anything personally. Daily life can be as separate or connected as desired. If you are sharing space

without a separate entrance, with family who want to cast you in the role of permanent babysitter, your independence may be at stake. Try simply being at home less. Consider volunteering for a month or two with an organization that offers housing and take a longer travel route to allow for a small amount of separation. Economical travel is available by train, plane, or bus. You need not own a car. Upon your return, attitudes will be renewed. If this is not an option, visit with friends or volunteer locally.

- **Inquire about Singles' Groups.** Attend seminars on subjects that interest you. If your income and social circle are limited, attend meals prepared for senior citizens living alone. Meals frequently come with a planned social activity. You may even find a new friendship as a surprise dessert!

- **Alternative Housing**. An economical park trailer, marketed under various names, is becoming popular with mature adult. This is a 400-square foot movable cottage designed for recreational use which may be towed or parked. Investigate www.RPTIA.com . There may be associated fees. It is also interesting to view ads for retirement communities depicting smiling couples holding hands, riding in golf carts or cruising in a boat or walking along a wooded trail. If you are considering a retirement community, check the median age; swim in the pool; ask if exercise facilities are co-ed; observe the environment. Is it more like an assisted living facility than an active community? Check social interaction, monthly maintenance fees (along with the rate of increase over the past five years), investigate rules and attitudes. Ownership of a private dwelling is different from living in a community where conformity may be dictated. Consider a trial year before committing to purchase. If you are looking to leave a snowy state behind, the climate should not be the only consideration. What about the distance from family and friends and travel costs? Consider your age, driving skills, car expenses, insurance, etc. Is there public transportation should you decide not to drive?

- **Open Road**. Many retirees choose to sell their home and purchase a travel vehicle. They head to warmer climes, dreamed-of locations, or simply drive off into the sunset to enjoy freedom without constraints. Whether it's a small pop-up trailer for short jaunts or a 40' condo-on-wheels, this mode of living is very popular. You may pick and choose locations at will, though fuel and maintenance costs may be an issue. RVing is a "turtle" lifestyle. Your home is ready to plug into conveniences whenever or wherever. You might choose to volunteer as a host at a national or state park. This entails meeting, greeting and perhaps housekeeping. Investigate through any national or state park web site. Church organizations frequently utilize RV'ers and Nomads for specific projects. Google for information on hosting and/or hook-up costs (see A-Z grid at the back of this book).

- **Loners on Wheels**: a single's group organized in 1969. Recognizing the need for a different type of singles club, the founder met with a group of other single campers in Death Valley, California. Check rules online. A yearly fee is charged which includes a monthly newsletter (see A-Z grid at the back of this book). 4Workampers travel country-wide in their RVs supplementing income by working part-time or in seasonal jobs at resorts, amusement parks in small towns and cities for $7-$12 per hour (see A-Z grid at the back of this book).
- **Full-time Retiree Volunteers** move from assignment to assignment; an alternative lifestyle with or without permanent housing offering freedom and independence (like me!).

The options listed in this chapter are but a few of the many that are available. As I have said, retirement takes a positive attitude and diligent research of options. Once you choose a course of action, you are off on a new adventure. Investigate, and most of all, enjoy!

Why Frank and Norma Jean volunteer ....

In 1997 this couple wanted to retire and hit the road. They sold their Iowa home on the river, bought an RV and soon found a spot where they could park the motor home during the Iowa summer to visit with friends, enjoy the weather and fishing, then volunteer during the rest of the year.

As Frank says, "We put eighty-three thousand miles on our rig and have been to every state. We enjoy being Nomads. Each volunteer location offers hook-ups and a purpose." Working in the home restoration business for twenty-four years, Frank gained a multitude of skills in general construction and property repair projects. Frank and I spoke in River Ridge, Louisiana, at the Little Farms United Church of Christ church hall.

He leaned back in his chair and chuckled. "My health was being compromised. The doctor told me to reduce my stress. I love working with people. Volunteering allows that and fun too!" Frank feels that having the freedom to travel while volunteering has been a positive change. Norma Jean, his pleasant counterpart, feels that volunteering offers, "A chance to be together away from the cold, to travel and enjoy great conversations with so many people. We haven't had any bad experiences. We choose a place where we've not been!"

Frank supervises construction while Norma Jean helps as needed at the church. Two years ago, the UCC needed a project leader. It was a position tailor-made for Frank. The couple now volunteers six months of each year. As Frank says, "This lifestyle suits us. It's our way of giving back."

Frequently Asked Questions

1. **Where/How do I find out about independent living options?** *Start at the local Senior Center. Peruse bulletin boards, check the phone book, ask questions and search the web. Check organizations like AARP or retirement magazines. In these times of national insecurity, isn't it a little dangerous to invite roommates or borders? Perhaps, but if you desire to stay in a family home and a roommate is the only option, require references and follow up on them. When interviewing, include a trusted friend. Perhaps discuss a short-term lease (six months) as a trial period.*

2. **How can we find exact costs of owning an RV?** *Attend local RV shows. Dealers are great for specifications on vehicles but they are there to sell. For "on the road" experiences, ask those who travel. Check Internet sites and blogs for current comments and tips from seasoned RVers.*

Interview: Betty

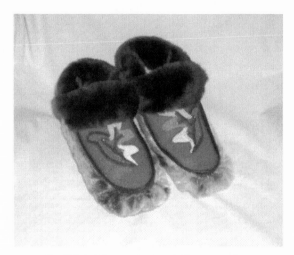

Sealskin Moccasins with Beaver trim;
Klingit leaf pattern, Spring/Summer/Fall/Winter

Betty .... *teacher, woodworker, wife, mother, sister, tractor driver and volunteer.*

"As iron sharpens iron, one man sharpens another."
-Proverb 27-17

"They called my car measles because it was so rusted," Betty laughed, "but, it got me and the students up and down the mountain roads."

After receiving her teaching degree in the 1940s, Betty volunteered to teach in the mountains of Phelps, Kentucky, smack in the middle of Hatfield-McCoy hollers. Back then, due to distance, mountain children did not attend public schools. If not for church-associated volunteer teachers like Betty, these children would not have received any education at all.

Betty told the following story about those days. "One night while teaching a Bible Study class in the church hall, I noticed faces appearing and disappearing in the windows; heard nothing, but felt a presence loitering as it got dark. I had heard about the boys who frightened off new teachers this way so when it was time to go, I quickly stuffed the children into the car for the ride home."

After dropping the last one off, Betty said that a car without headlights chased her up one holler and down another. "Don't know how I lost them! But, I had hiked those mountains and knew where I was going." (Betty had earned the name mountain goat from her journeys up and down and around to teach.) "Just after I lost them, Measles stalled—out of gas. I managed to call a friend and was pushed home. I guess someone was watching over us."

As a young girl, Betty had two favorite pastimes, flying a kite in the brisk Missouri wind, and listening to Bible stories. "We would gather up close as Mrs. Robb, the minister's wife, would read story after story to the primary Sunday School class. One day while reading, Mrs. Robb paused to ask, do you children know there are boys and girls around the world who have not heard these stories?"

Betty was astonished. It seemed incredible to her that some children would not hear the stories she took for granted and vowed she would do whatever possible so that all children would hear the stories she loved. Little did she know that those same stories would remain in her heart, fueling her compassion throughout her adult life.

As a one-room schoolteacher in the hollers, Betty often "visited" families, handling many grade levels simultaneously. She remembers how on one particular summer day she was sitting under a tree barefoot, reading. "I heard 'clop, clop, clop' on the road. I looked up and saw a handsome young man who lived over the next hill, standing in a cart, his mule plodding along, head bobbing with each step." She looked. He looked back. She thought, "Hmm, I think that family needs to be visited."

Why Betty volunteers .... "There are so many reasons," Betty explained. "One is because I want to be useful. I want to make my time count while I am in this world. But, another reason is my Aunt Pauline who used to make popcorn for us as children. When the popcorn began to pop on the stove, we would dance to the rhythm, hopping and twirling around the kitchen." Smiling, Betty murmured, "Aunt Pauline always said, keep yourself busy helping others and you won't have time to feel sorry for yourself."

Bernard and Betty were married in 1955 at her home-town Missouri Range Line church. Returning to Kentucky, just when Betty thought her life was perfect, Bernard was drafted. He encouraged her return to Missouri. "You can't stay here by yourself!" he said. It did not matter that she had traveled to school in Mississippi by herself when young women did not attend school away from home. It did not matter that she had gone to Kentucky by herself, had walked up and down the hollers by herself. Suddenly she could not stay by herself now that her husband might be shipped out?

Dutifully she returned to the family homestead to care for two elderly uncles. This eventually led her to adopt a farming lifestyle. Farming is similar to volunteering in that you do what is expected with pleasure. We who do not participate in the all-consuming 24/7 pace of life on a farm sometimes take for granted what it takes to get our milk, vegetables and meat.

At a County Fair in Okeechobee, Florida, I spoke with four young women who raise heifers, doing whatever it takes to insure their health to produce the best product for the market. These animals are livestock, not pets. Such is the nature of farming. Raising an animal or any farm product entails an enormous amount of personal dedication.

As Betty says, "Farming has been in our family for seven generations. It is in our blood, our way of life. Caring for the land and animals comes naturally."

Betty's Personal Projects and How Everyone Can Help.

- **Pet Project**. PET is an acronym for Personal Energy Transport, a volunteer organization based in Columbia, Missouri. They make a "hand-cranked, three-wheeled, sturdy and maintainable wheelchair capable of traveling rough trails, with hauling capability" to aid those with disabilities, thus lifting them into a productive life of hope and dignity. There is a long list of dedicated volunteers who help make these vehicles, paying most of the cost themselves. Betty makes the chair backs, sanding, routing, painting and stenciling, before delivering them to the assembly area near her home in Missouri. She enjoys participating in this "gift of mobility" for individuals at home and abroad.
- **JARRS.** This is a linguistics training school that translates the Bible into native languages. A dream of a "missionary aviation service" evolved

into JARRS, the Jungle Aviation and Radio Service, an organization that originated in Peru with one airplane, and continues at the JAARS Center in Waxhaw, NC. Betty provided support services at the center, nestling her tiny pop-up trailer amongst the 42' RVs in the parking area. At JAARS, volunteers pay their own way; providing their own housing and food; donating their services to those translating or preparing for overseas assignments.

- **Habitat for Humanity**. Betty was assigned to work with a crew scheduled to begin building a home in Sedalia, Missouri. She arrived early, saw no one, so started hauling brush. Others came along, but she did not think it was a big deal starting alone. As she says, "It was just another project that needed doing."
- **CROP**. The Community Hunger Appeal of Church World Service is comprised of dedicated volunteers who provide goods or services to help fight hunger. While raising her children, Betty heard that CROP needed quilters. She does not know how many she made, but since the proceeds would be used to fight hunger, stitching became a labor of love.

Note: Web addresses of the above are listed in the A-Z grid in the back of this book.

Notes on Volunteering .... At the college in Sitka, volunteers were given three meals a day during the week and on Saturday, and two on Sunday, brunch and dinner. When the college was closed between semesters, volunteers were on their own for meals, but a grocery store was not far away and each residence had a communal kitchen. Volunteers accumulated two days off per month, which could be taken at their own discretion as long as it did not cause any disruption within their responsibilities. Organizations utilizing volunteers routinely offer earned time off to long-term volunteers. If certain benefits are expected or it is important that accustomed amenities are available, be certain to ask the Volunteer Coordinator if they do exist as part of the volunteer program.

Volunteering in Alaska was something Betty never expected to do. She heard about the opportunity through her church and drove to Sitka with her pop-up camper hitched to her van, prepared to camp along the way to save money. This is not the sort of thing most seventy-five year old women do.

While at Sheldon Jackson College in Sitka, Betty worked in housekeeping and the cafeteria, waking at 5:00 a.m. every morning to greet those coming for breakfast. She resided in single women housing (as I did), on the second floor of the Administrative Building, in a corner room overlooking the Sitka Marina and Mount Edgecombe. Her sewing machine was placed on a table in the corner, ready for action.

On icy mornings, Betty used moose tracks, a spiked apparatus strapped onto her shoes or boots. With sure footing, she was off early, often returning late from her appointed rounds.

In Sitka, the State Trooper Barracks is adjacent to the college and troopers-in-training eat their meals in the cafeteria. Every morning these focused young Alaskan residents would file by the registration desk with a few brisk, but friendly, words. Betty heard one of the troopers was expecting triplets and she knew money was tight. Although busy sewing curtains, folding laundry, and other tasks, Betty canvassed for donations. At graduation, she quietly presented this unsolicited helping-hand.

Volunteering as a housekeeper is hard work. Betty stripped beds and piled the dirty linen onto an old-fashioned wooden cart with two bicycle wheels. She'd then drag it to the laundry area, unload, wash, dry and refold before piling all into the cart for the trip back to a laundry closet on each floor of a dorm or guest room area. It would be strenuous work for someone younger, but she persevered with passionate dedication.

Betty felt the Guest House on campus was pretty dilapidated. "Not welcoming at all," she frowned. She took it upon herself to paint, sew drapes, and supplement the meager furnishings with matching bedspreads from the "White E.", a thrift shop in Sitka staffed by volunteers that raise thousands of dollars for various charity efforts. That guest house sparkled!

Betty utilized her woodworking skills to create chandeliers for the local Presbyterian Church. The only help she needed was hanging them since they were too heavy to lift over her head! At the end of her volunteer assignment, she brought home Alaska-themed material to make yet another quilt to be auctioned in the fall at the local "Festival of Sharing". As usual, a portion of the proceeds from the quilt will be designated for Heifer International.

On her driving alone to Alaska, she said, "People have said that I was brave, but not really. I just got into my camper and drove. It was exciting!"

Now Betty is content to work at home, happily married to a home-town friend. She has put aside the PET Project but continues to sponsor a young woman orphaned and displaced by conflict in Kenya. She makes jellies, pickles and preserves for a yearly county-wide church fair whose proceeds contribute to help end poverty and hunger. Her stitching of quilts keeps young and old warm on the coldest nights, at home and abroad.

According to Betty, the future is open to our helping one another and feels that education is the key. She intends to keep working until she cannot.

I can see her approaching the Pearly Gates, asking, "Is there anything I can do?"

Betty's active participation in the five stages of retirement:

1. **Imagination**—*imagining herself as a teacher catalyzed her courage to complete one goal after another, right up to retirement. Courage spurs Betty's imagination;*
2. **Anticipation**—*raising two children and caring for her husband and mother while managing their farm;*
3. **Liberation**—*driving to volunteer at JAARS;*
4. **Transition**—*hearing of the opportunity in Alaska—leasing her farm land—driving to Sitka;*
5. **Reconciliation**—*enjoyment in volunteering; the PET Project; quilts for CROP; canning vegetables and fruits for Harvest Festivals, enabling a constant supply of healthy food for her community. All donated with compassion.*

FIVE:

Guilt Wilts

> *"There are two kinds of light - the glow that illuminates, and the glare that obscures."* James Thurber, writer and cartoonist (1894-1961)

Adult child-parent relationships are like the animal in the Dr. Doolittle books for children, the pushmi-pullyu. A craving for security pulls family members together while the need for independence pushes them away from each other. As adolescents, we are anxious to be independent, yet as the years pass, sometimes we dread the very independence we help our children seek, leading to guilt.

Guilt is a cumbersome, internal moral conflict. Prior to retirement, response was to the urgency of another person's needs and desires with automatic compliance—an almost reflexive response to pressure. But now that there is time, there is the luxury of being able to consider what you want.[3] Tread lightly. Like any piece of heavy baggage, guilt can cause you to lose your balance.

We experience guilt every day. It pesters us while we eat that chocolate donut; pokes at us for not meeting a deadline or because there is a need to work instead of being a stay-at-home parent. Insufficient time to complete necessary tasks at home or in the community can cause anxiety, discouragement, and frustration.

When we commit to a responsibility, the intention is to complete the given task, but sometimes life interrupts. It could be that due to a sick parent

---

3   Emotional Blackmail, Susan Forward, Ph.D., Chapter 9, Pg. 171, (HarperCollins Publisher 1977)

we have less time. Perhaps income is necessary and work takes precedent, or maybe the task itself becomes more demanding than anticipated or we become frustrated with the projected outcome. Frustration develops when we attempt to squeeze twenty-seven hours of activity into the twenty-four we are given each day.

Freda ... dynamo, nurse, writer, voracious reader and volunteer explaining why she chose to travel straight to a new assignment without returning home first.

"I had been away for ten years," Freda said, feigning exasperation, "and they thought I would return to the family fold. They just did not understand. I can't get enough of new things to do, places to go, and people to meet. In the end, they weren't too disappointed because now they could tell their friends about their weird mother. People would ask and my kids would tell them where I'd gone. 'Wow,' they would say, your mother sure gets around."

Guilt surfaces when we perceive a gap between what we strive to be and who we think we are. When it appears, we must challenge the voice of insecurity and overcome the roadblocks of those who discourage our dreams for (perhaps) selfish reasons.

Work on generating pride in your goals or decisions. This will ease fears and make transition easier. Share the pleasure of your retirement with others so that the simple joy and enthusiasm of each decision you make will be apparent. Assure everyone that postcards from each destination will be on the top of your to-do list.

Our lives are governed by lists. We make grocery lists and errand lists. We scribble hasty lists while driving, and often misplace them when rushing around frazzled. Arriving at a destination, the first thing we reach for is our list—that is if we remember where we put it. Each list is prioritized, often with asterisks placed next to perceived priorities.

In retirement, what is your first priority? Think about it. What should be listed prior to dreams, schemes or goals? On my retirement list, I placed my name at the top. After all, this is my new lifestyle.

A list of priorities is a must when thinking about retirement. The list may contain projected deadlines or dreams, housing options and finances, but should begin with the name of the person who is about to step into retirement.

Insights from Freda

"If someone had told me I would be volunteering at eighty, I would have told them they were crazy!" She smiled, dismissing the idea that her stamina was anything special.

"When I arrived in Utah, the President at the university handling the volunteer program asked, 'How old are you?' Thinking that it was none of his business how old I am, I answered, I am seventy-six and starting a new life!" Freda shrugged. *"I knew I was qualified for the position or VISTA would not have sent me. How dare he question my motives, or my age? I was there, happy, and ready to begin my adventure as the family nurse on the Ute Reservation. I stayed for two paid years, and eight non-paid. Guess I showed him what an older woman could do!"*

One of the most difficult hurdles a retiree has to overcome is the negative reaction of family when they are informed of future plans. There may be shock, disbelief, or even disapproval, depending on what the retiree professes to do, or where they wish to go.

The idea of a parent taking off to volunteer in an unfamiliar place or interacting with strangers may be perceived as irresponsible. If a retiree's choice is to travel in an RV with no permanent address, friends might wonder if they are "running away." Adult children may be shocked at a parent's craving for space— emotional or physical. Neighbors may encourage, albeit a bit wistful, or even secretly jealous. After all, doesn't everyone need a place to come back to?

Respond, don't react. Remain positive in the face of negativity. Control your emotions and reserve judgment. Do not alter your plans. Give the teapot time to brew. You may be surprised at the result.

What if the situation were reversed? What if an adult child were offered a job opportunity elsewhere? In considering whether to accept, the child would list priorities, and if parents appeared on the list at all it would most likely be an afterthought. They certainly would not be first. The expectation would be that they would celebrate the child's good fortune.

When a child follows their dream, they are to be congratulated. Yet, if a parent wants to pursue their dream in retirement, it is questioned. As we live our lives, our dreams accumulate, and we want the freedom to pursue them without criticism. We expect our adult children to act like adults when we inform them of our plans. When this does not happen, we ask, "Am I being selfish?" No. At this stage of life it is not selfish to put yourself first.

However, at the onset of their parents' retirement, adult children may have certain expectations which they may or may not have shared. Communication is essential. Surprises are not usually welcome and can backfire if not presented appropriately. Reaction to the unexpected can be ugly.

A volunteer retirement lifestyle is an opportunity to utilize parental skills of patience and flexibility. Prior to making any announcement to your family, list the whys and wherefores behind your choices so that you may articulate your objectives clearly. Whatever the dream, unless your goals are obedient to your inner voice, some form of regret (however fleeting) might surface. I have made it a rule to go with my first thought. No second-guessing over the age of sixty-five!

Freda begins her volunteer career...

"We raised our family in Chicago," Freda said. "I worked as a nurse and newspaper reporter. My husband was a doctor and between his salary and mine, we led good life, but when he died unexpectedly, it was up to me to make our dreams come true. All our lives, we had talked about a retirement life of travel and volunteer medical service around the world, but now I was alone. I applied to the Peace Corps as a Registered Nurse and was accepted and given an assignment to Morocco.

However, my son intervened. He had been in the Peace Corps in Liberia and warned me off going to Morocco. 'No, no, no! Arab men do not treat women well,' he said.

At the time I deferred to his judgment." Freda burst out laughing. "I'm not quite sure I would do so now!"

At least one year prior to retirement, begin by having a conversation with immediate family about your thoughts. Let them know what might happen, what the future might hold, and revisit that conversation every two months prior to a projected retirement date.

Do not keep your plans a secret. If objections are voiced, counter them with logic. Silence denotes conformity. Do not allow your family to assume you will be available to them during retirement when your desire is to volunteer or travel. If you were planning a vacation, you would certainly notify everyone concerned and share your excitement with them. Retirement is a vacation of sorts. It may be structured or unstructured, with or without an alarm clock, with or without definite parameters. Your family cannot be aware of your ideas and plans if not shared.

Volunteering is infectious. Compassion spreads like ripples on water, gently touching others. Sometimes the effects are obvious. Sometimes the impact goes unrecognized until much later. A volunteer retiree becomes an example to imitate, a role model. Each time a volunteer destination is chosen, life begins anew. As long as your actions are responsible, your goals remain in focus, and your enjoyment is visible, you are guaranteed to have a positive impact on those around you.

Surveys indicate that single women are the most likely to volunteer. This does not mean single men are not out there serving with equal zeal and compassion. It is simply that women are caretakers. With them, filling a need is second-nature.

Perhaps this is why "empty-nest syndrome" hits women the hardest. They tend to blame themselves for past issues that should be forgotten or forgiven. They have trouble moving on, therefore enabling children who should be independent.

This happens to both mothers and fathers. Guilt-ridden parents should be strong enough to maintain a life that is separate from those who would continue to be dependent on them. This is easy to say. Be strong in your decisions. Guilt needs no reinforcement.

Men do not seem to bear the burden of guilt the way women do. Guilt is not always obvious. It often appears in disguise, subtle, like hesitation to change, or an impulse to cling to the status quo. Acknowledging an empty nest allows for a change of lifestyle, more free time, and perhaps more disposable income. Of course, if adult children are yo-yo's scratch that. I am referring to children who bounce back and forth between dependence and independence, moving out, moving back in, hoping to achieve some sort of resolution.

__Barbara on the road__ .... Driving through Canada and Alaska my out-of-state license plates would often raise eyebrows. Women were curious. Most men, as soon as they discovered I was driving solo, would find a reason to change the subject or simply walk away. My independence seemed to intimidate both sexes, yet the wives would linger to hear what I had to say. One, after looking around to see if her husband could overhear, whispered, "My husband would never let me drive alone!" She was interested, obviously envious of my solo adventures. Perhaps, someday, she will lose the guilt and act on her desires.

This puts a strain on all involved and might be a good time to find a place to volunteer for a few months. It is amazing how quickly adult children mature when parents are not around to enable them. By the time they reach retirement, whenever possible, parents should be focused on themselves.

We love our children and grandchildren, but as we grow from one phase of life to another, there comes a time when children should be thought of as descendants not dependents. This does not mean estrangement. It simply means they are no longer dependent on you for survival.

I raised my children with the philosophy, be responsible for yourself before attempting to be responsible for someone else. Function as a single, independent person before you try to provide materially or financially for someone else. Families begin with singles joining together, one becoming two, two becoming three or four or more. As the years pass, the three or more revert to two, or one. Practice responsibility to self, to mankind, and to the environment. Focus on your retirement encourages others to focus on their lives.

Retirement is a time to dispel the myths of aging. Today's retiree is not the same floundering soul of years past, the bespectacled granny with the towel apron or the pipe smoking, paper-reading front-porch grandpa. Seniors today remain involved because life continues to evolve. We must change with changing times.

Some of our parents never reached retirement age. Some, particularly those who suffered through the Depression, never even thought about retirement. Hunger and poverty are not easily forgotten. Caution ruled decisions. Likewise, retirement should be a deliberate step. It should be a state of mind that comes into focus gradually. Keep your mind on the process, what to do, where to go, who to meet, not the outcome. This is how those empty hours will remain filled.

Our adult children sometimes suffer from separation anxiety. Retirees can too. Talk it out, smooth it out, and then, get out. Remember that volunteering can be scheduled, like a vacation, for everyone's convenience. You can be home for six months, away for six, or home for eleven, away for one, whatever fits. With today's technology, accessibility is a mere cell phone call away, complete with video.

Attention Required

Before beginning any short-term or long-term volunteer adventure, there are items that require attention. The process involves more than arranging for mail pick-up or pet sitting:

- Contemplate – Consider your choice, and ponder the effect on yourself and others.
- Research – Be sensitive to culture and environment at your chosen destination. If leaving for another country, make time to learn as much as you can.
- Assure —Be ready to deal with any situation mentally and physically. Maintain links to family and friends through snail-mail, e-mail and cell phone. If exercise is important, check accessibility to exercise at your destination.
- Anticipate —It may be necessary to live without services such as Internet, laundry, even running water. Should any of the above become more than a simple inconvenience, discuss and resolve with coordinators. If leaving the country, check with doctors for immunizations or booster shots.
- Forecast—Estimate the cost of travel and personal expenditures, even overestimate. The best way to manage is with an ATM card. Also, keep all receipts for the IRS if reimbursement is desired. Leave an itinerary with family and friends. If joining a volunteer group with a trip planner, keep in close contact for pertinent information on your destination.

- Remember—When appropriate, take along items which may be more expensive or difficult to obtain at your destination. If you have a specific need, do not assume it will be available. Remember medications. Make copies of important documents, including Advance Directives, to store separately in luggage or leave behind with family should they be lost or stolen. If you are driving, notify insurance agent(s) of destination and length of assignment. Remember batteries and printer paper. Shopping is not always convenient.
- Notify—Consider how long you will be away. Alert neighbors, arrange for lawn care, pet care, mail pick-up or complete a temporary change of address card signifying start and stop dates at the post office.
- Include—Pack a sense of humor and optimism along with your passion for volunteering! Leave pride, self-righteousness, and attitude at home. Take along a healthy container of humility, open-mindedness, curiosity and compassion. Consider climate and weather conditions and plan accordingly. Minimize baggage. Remember, volunteer housing may not offer a convenient washer and dryer or sufficient storage.

Despite precautions, family relationships may suffer when a retiree leaves for a long-term assignment. One way to deal with this for those under ten is to purchase a map and outline the route indicating landmarks and scheduled stops and circle the destination. For adults, discuss, highlighting what you plan to do and see. Let all share in your excitement.

In the 1990s, prior to my retirement, I worked in Hawaii for five years. I was worried that being so far away would harm my fledgling relationship with my (then) six-month-old granddaughter. I devised a method of keeping in touch by creating videos of interesting places, speaking with her or reading books to her. It worked!

The videos encouraged a feeling of togetherness although the distance was considerable. Upon my return to the mainland, I developed my ideas about keeping in touch into a brochure which I used as the basis for an Adult Education class. This method proved that there are ways to maintain relationships while living elsewhere, even if your visits are sporadic.

Keeping in Touch

- Communication is imperative: maintain communication on a weekly basis, not just an occasional letter, package or card for birthdays or holidays. A weekly reminder, even something as simple as a postcard, reinforces a relationship. Communication may be simple and inexpensive, but it must be consistent—something, a card or letter or email, once a week, every week. Skype once a month. It does wonders for all involved, and it works! Once a routine is established, cut back to every other week if you wish.

- Correspondence for those under ten-years-old: with a digital camera, simply take a self-portrait and cut/paste it onto a document as letterhead. Type, print or handwrite your greeting. When the young person opens the envelope or box, the first thing they will see is your face. This cements familiarity via association. Option: If you don't have a digital camera, use a photo of yourself. Cut it to size, place it face down on any copier (check the local library) place a piece of plain paper over the photo and press copy to print a page of "personal stationery." If possible, include the recipient in the picture so that when the mail is opened both faces will be visible.

- How-to make your own VIDEO or DVD: Remember when you were a child and someone said, "Come sit, read with me. What treasures we will find...." Keeping in touch reinforces that memory and shares it with someone else. Using a camcorder or cell phone, videotape any location or site of interest. I chose Sea World, filming what I thought would be of interest. At times, I sat and spoke directly to my granddaughter, explaining what would come next. When finished, I packed the video into a box with her birthday present and mailed it. My son called to express his delight. "She loves it," he said, "but she keeps fast-forwarding to your face. Can you do something with just you?" What an assignment! So, at the library I checked-out three books that I knew were on her bookshelf. Then, I bought a new book which would be a surprise. Positioning myself on the couch, I aimed the camcorder in my direction and announced, "Hi! Today we will read Mike Mulligan and Mary Ann. Grab a chair and sit down so we can read together." The process continued for four years.

79

- Steps to making a reading DVD are as follows: Purchase book(s) for your recipient's age group, or borrow some from the library. Access a camcorder or rent one for the day or use your smart phone. Position the camcorder yourself or have a friend video you. Make yourself comfortable on the couch or chair. Begin filming; Introduce yourself and the book. If your viewer already has the book, allow time for retrieval; Begin to read. Also try reading short stories for older bed-ridden friends. Being read to is appreciated; it is a luxury seldom found; When finished filming, pack up the DVD/video, along with the new book, and mail it to that "special" recipient. Yes, snail mail. Some things cannot be done by email (unless your grandchildren have a Kindle.
- Options for adults: "Let's spend some time together...." Distant family or friends may enjoy a more personal type of communication, something more than letters or postcards. Again, make a video. Film a tourist site, play with a dog, tour a garden; walk in the woods or on the beach. Film places the recipient may remember. One woman I know videoed her garden, describing each flower, then sat on a bench and read a book. She packed the video with the book and sent it to her mother in a long-term-care facility.
- Options for adolescents: Purchase a small photo album. Take photos of landmarks or places of interest. Print pictures and match each photo with an informational index card. The recipient may then peruse at leisure. Include a map for visual reference. My travel photo albums have been used for show-and tell and geography class. You may also be able to make an on-line album if your student's class has AV access.

Oh, the places Freda went and the things she did .... *After living and working on the Ute Reservation for a few years, Freda wanted change. She found a trailer in the town of Bluff, Utah, 20 minutes from Blanding and the clinic. She resided there for eight more years as Health Nurse for the reservation. "I was useful and content," she said. "I had a home, didn't need to go anywhere to find one. I lived close enough to the Ute and Navajo Rez to be friendly with both."*

Around 1996, Freda mentioned her interest in Alaska to Ameri-Corps. Within three days she heard back, packed, and was gone. "In Sitka, I did a jazz show at the NPR radio station and wrote for the newspaper, but my main volunteer responsibility was at the battered women and children's clinic. I cherish my Tlingit sisters. I wish I'd helped even more than I did. Alaskan culture is a difficult issue for native women and men today. We need to show patience and kindness."

Nearing ninety, Freda listened to her son and lived at an assisted living facility in Chicago where she kept busy writing a column for the newspaper dedicated to all 'adult youths'. "I would sing and dance," she said, "and they think I'm weird. That's nothing new. My family is glad that I'm nearby, but if my health was good, I'd be off like a shot, even if my son said no!"

Note: But that didn't last long. Today, Freda is back in Alaska, living independent as she always wanted to be. Someday, (as she says) it will be "my time", but it will be "my way".

Practicing keeping in touch allows for instant recognition upon your return. Busy lives do not provide leeway for attention to relationships. Consistent communication is essential. A grandparent relationship differs from that of parent/ child. The role of grandparent allows for flexibility in responsibility. This translates to fun and a cross-generational closeness which cannot be explained. The experience is priceless.

If or when retirement is imminent, guilt should not be part of the agenda. Attempt to:

- Live happily in the moment.
- Communicate your goals and share your experiences.
- Find ways to accommodate family celebrations while attending to your volunteer responsibilities. Offer a train or plane ticket to where you are as a birthday present to a grandchild so they may share the volunteer experience with you.
- Encourage family to include your volunteer destination as part of their vacation. Everyone benefits.
- Guard against negative stress as it takes a toll on the body as well as the mind.
- Enjoy new found freedom without the extra baggage of guilt.

Frequently Asked Questions

1. How did you convince your family that you would be safe driving alone?
First, it was not necessary to convince anyone or ask permission to pursue my objective. My family is accustomed to my stubborn independence. However, I am not so confident that I do not take necessary steps of caution. Let your wisdom shine through your enthusiasm.

2. How did your grandchildren react? They thought it was "cool" until they heard I would be away for a year. We talked and I left a map, even planned phone-call visits (school made travel impossible). They were excited.

3. While away for that year, upon return, did your grandchildren really remember you? Yes. When I returned, they brought out the postcards I sent them and asked me to explain places, people, events. "Maybe you can take me next time?" they asked. The key is consistency. Planned communication, even something as simple as a postcard, triggers familiarity. To this day, I send postcards every other week. My grandchildren enjoy that!

Interview: Sue and Terry

Menaul School, Albuquerque, NM

Sue ... *teacher and librarian, wife, mother, storyteller, and volunteer.*

Terry ... *banker, teacher, husband and father, painter, entertainer, and volunteer.*

Sue

"My first introduction to long-distance volunteering was as a bride in Iran." Sue spoke softly, relating the chaotic experience of combining marriage and the desire to teach in Iran for three years. At that time, Sue was married to Dennis.

"We were so naïve and anxious to serve. We were enjoying our teaching experience when my husband received his draft notice," she said, belying the trepidation she must have felt at the time. "Since I was pregnant and did not want to remain in Iran alone, we decided to return to the United States. We were in Denmark—halfway home with our belongings on the container ship—when we received the news that Dennis had been given a deferment. Not a grand way to end our quest! But, I knew there would be other chances."

Sue and Dennis eventually settled in Morgantown, West Virginia, where their family now numbered five. During her mothering days, Sue volunteered in the ways many young parents volunteer, but with a twist. Since they lived in a college community, foreign students were included in their family activities. Sue felt strongly that her children should be exposed to other cultures. She welcomed these students through the Rotary Exchange Program and Council of International Programs.

When her oldest child was about to graduate from high school, Sue turned to substitute teaching, discovering that she enjoyed working with deaf children. She took a course in American Sign Language, but since West Virginia University at Morgantown did not offer education for deaf children as a major, Sue decided to return to school for a master's of library science.

***Why Sue volunteers …… ***"It's my belief that one should tithe their time as well as their finances. With a young family it is impossible, but if we assume our lifespan is close to 100 years, and if we can volunteer approximately 10 years, we will have tithed our time. That is sort of my goal. If I can do more, fine and dandy. Also, volunteering at places offering room and board helps your retirement money stretch farther."*

It was during these busy years that Sue's father died and her mother, who had volunteered throughout her life, relocated to Morgantown to take a position as House Mother at a local college sorority. This decision would prove propitious, for Sue's life was about to change radically. In January, 2000, Dennis died from heart surgery complications. This trauma turned her family upside-down.

Sue recovered slowly from the depths of sadness and loss. A year passed before she could investigate volunteering options. Since her children were now grown, she thought it might be time for new places and new faces. Her mother mentioned Menaul, a college prep school in Albuquerque, New Mexico, suggesting that Sue might enjoy volunteering there.

Sue remembered befriending a couple from Guatemala who moved to Morgantown so the husband could attend orthodontics school. "They lived near us and it seemed natural to assist the young wife in adjusting to her new environment—shopping, schools, language—relocation ins-and-outs." A few years later, the Guatemala couple had moved to Albuquerque, and so now Sue thought, "Albuquerque might be nice." There was a lot to consider with selling her home and downsizing to an apartment which provided a home base that was smaller and more manageable.

She applied to Menaul and other volunteer destinations, but when the school called to offer a volunteer position working in the library, she accepted. Sue was thrilled to reconnect with her Guatemalan friends and be back in a library environment. Menaul School wanted her to come for a full semester, but she negotiated a two-month stay through the Volunteer Coordinator. They accepted her conditions with the promise that she would consider returning for longer the next school year. Soon she was on her way to New Mexico, expecting to spend a few months in the Southwest, and return to Morgantown.

In January, Sue left 70° temperatures in West Virginia, to arrive to snow in Albuquerque!

It was a reminder that nature, and life, may not meet expectations.

Sue's active participation in the five stages of retirement

1. **Imagination**—*Investigates volunteer options to regain her sense of self;*
2. **Anticipation**—*Reduces her footprint; downsizing before leaving for New Mexico;*
3. **Liberation**—*Chooses Menaul School as her first long-distance volunteer experience;*
4. **Transition**—*Recognizing the desire to find a new direction, Sue contributes her skills and enjoys her new surroundings;*
5. **Reconciliation**—*A continued pursuit, with Terry, to be happy in their volunteer lifestyle.*

Terry

Meanwhile, Terry was in Fort Wayne, Indiana, attempting to start over after a divorce, wondering what direction his life should take. "I had heard about a volunteer opportunity at Menaul School in New Mexico," he said with a laugh.. "It was a chance to contribute my skills in a new environment."

Why Terry volunteers .... *"I was at a fork in the road, alone and* *without purpose. Volunteering was a natural course for me to pursue offering countless opportunities to learn and serve—and, I met Sue!"*

Terry became an assistant to the Director of Admissions at Menaul. He felt comfortable in the loving, accepting atmosphere. "I found myself surrounded by youth, busy with work I enjoyed, co-mingling with passionate and purposeful co-workers," he said. "Life, while not exactly complete, was good."

Friendships blossomed in the small comfortable house he shared with other volunteers. For six years, Terry, with his accommodating manner and quick smile, contributed his skills in Admissions and Financial Aid. "I especially enjoyed learning the names of the students, greeting many of them every morning," he said with a sigh as pleasant memories surfaced. Although the nature of his position did not allow direct interaction with the students after enrollment, this small but important gesture lead to many expressions of gratitude at graduation.

Terry's active participation in the five stages of retirement

1. **Imagination**—*Exited the stressful banking arena to form his own House Painting business;*
2. **Anticipation**—*While recovering from divorce, he considered options to relocate and volunteer;*
3. **Liberation**—*Spent six years at Menaul School regaining his self-worth while contributing skills, camaraderie and compassion;*
4. **Transition**—*Terry met Sue, combining goals and resources to spend their lives together;*
5. **Reconciliation**—*Continued pursuit, with Sue, to be happy in their volunteer lifestyle.*

Sue and Terry

"While Terry was transitioning to Menaul," Sue explained, "my grown children were diversifying. One son moved to Wisconsin, my daughter remained in West Virginia and my oldest married and moved to Africa!"

Sue was learning that if we are patient, some of life's unfairness dissipates. Upon arrival at Menaul School she was assigned to the same house Terry occupied with one other woman volunteer, sharing experiences, working toward a common goal.

"At spring break," Sue said, "when I was scheduled to return home, the three us had made plans to visit Lake Powell. I had forgotten the school would be closed and my plane ticket had me there through the break."

At the last minute, the third member of the party canceled and Sue and Terry traveled together alone. During Elderhostel classes on Native American Culture and ecology of the area, they became better acquainted. When it came time for Sue to leave, both realized that friendship had turned to romance.

"Spending time apart was difficult," Terry recalled, "but we communicated by phone—a lot. When the school year ended, I scheduled a trip to West Virginia. Could not get there fast enough!"

They enjoyed the summer months, sharing their happiness with family and friends. While driving back to Menaul for the fall semester, the couple decided to marry during the holidays. At a rented cabin in a Maryland State Park, they were joined together in a delightfully simple ceremony performed by Sue's stepfather, a Presbyterian minister.

In January, 2003, they returned to Menaul to finish the year. After that, the couple returned to Morgantown and revived a previous desire to volunteer at Sheldon Jackson College in Sitka, Alaska.

"I served as Librarian," Sue said, "assuming front desk duties as well as working behind the scenes, locating information, and assisting students at the computers, while Terry, despite his skills in admissions and financial aid, worked for the college maintenance department."

Insight on the Job .... *At Menaul, Sue noticed that communal housing areas were not conducive to either conversation or watching TV. She had looked forward to viewing to the Winter Olympics, but not by herself. After a little discussion, Sue said, "we moved the furniture around to improve interaction, and our house at Menaul became a happier place." Terry countered. "In a diverse environment, you don't so much change others as they change you."*

Terry interrupted. "Marcel, the maintenance supervisor, needed workers desperately, especially painters. It was manual labor, climbing up and down ladders, lugging paint supplies, attending to small repairs when necessary, but I really enjoyed working at my own pace, and I am an experienced painter."

They were assigned a one-bedroom apartment in a communal setting with other couples and single males, along with three meals in the cafeteria. Sue entertained public and private groups with storytelling. "I really enjoyed the storytelling part," Sue said, "and we both enjoyed the hiking, kayaking, and interaction with fellow volunteers."

Terry, not to be outdone, teamed up with another volunteer to produce a slapstick skit entitled, "The Two Stooges," a sort of Harpo Marx meets Monte Python. It was performed at the Student Center, one of the many volunteer activities.

Before returning to the Lower 48 in 2007, the couple took a long deserved vacation, driving into the interior of Alaska. Back home in West Virginia, they learned that Sue's daughter was expecting twins, and so chose to volunteer at home in '08. "The library is much easier," Sue chuckled. "Books do not need to be fed and diapered."

"Very true," Terry said, nodding, "but how about I share something." He winked at Sue. "In '96, way before Sue and I met, I volunteered through Elderhostel at a Habitat for Humanity build in Georgia. After Sue and I married, I was packing some stuff before she and I drove back to Morgantown when I came across a picture of the Habitat group in Georgia and showed it to Sue. She stared at it. Her mother and step-father were in the group. Amazing! Through volunteering I met Sue's parents before I met her. Ironic, isn't it?" What does the future hold for Sue and Terry? This is open to discussion. Their families applaud their endeavors, and they do take time out to visit children and grandchildren, but service remains their primary focus.

"We enjoy long-term long-distance volunteering because by spending a longer period of time in the same place, we develop a more intimate relationship with the community," Sue said. "We are not there as tourists. We work, play, and enjoy while contributing."

"Besides," Terry smiled, "we can travel without worrying about paying rent, which is a big part of anyone's budget. Our skills are needed—here at home, or at Menaul, or in Alaska... or somewhere!"

Sue gave him a thoughtful look. "Let's get the twins up and walking first."

SIX:

Pleasure and Treasure

"While we try to teach our children about life, our children teach us what life is all about."
Angela Schwindt

Spiritual tranquility ... *The mystical sapphire surface mirrors lingering tufts of cottony clouds and ragged evergreen branches as dawn comes to Crater Lake. Caldera and creatures welcome fingers of warmth as sunbeams reach over mountain ridges. I sit on the edge of Sun Notch rim overlooking the Phantom Ship, my knees drawn to my chest, eyes closed. As the morning warbler sings, I allow my psyche to absorb the soothing powers of this magical place.*

Some of the pleasures of volunteering are as obvious as looking at a waterfall, or a crystal blue lake, or wildlife, offering an immediate impact of awe and excitement. Others may be invisible—at first.

Unexpected pleasures are usually subtle, surfacing as a chance encounter with a stranger who extends a welcome, or a detour which delays you from reaching your destination but provides you with a sunset you remember long afterward.

Whether alone or with someone else, wherever you are, pay attention to the moment, and take time for the unexpected. Stop to savor a deep breath as an eagle flies overhead. Notice the wingspan and the white head, how nonchalantly it soars. Slow down to enjoy a moment in the mountains, the first glimpse of a city skyline, a roadside break alone or with fellow travelers. Live as though you are not quite finished with life. Age hands us this privilege. No matter how many years we have accumulated, there is still much to do. The alternative allows plenty of time to rest.

Simple pleasures .... Fresh huckleberries picked early in the morning from the Farm Market in Missoula, Montana, stirred into yogurt—breakfast by the side of an effervescent mountain stream at the perimeter of Glacier Park, just before entering Canada.

And... with fellow volunteers, I scoop baby salmon in huge nets, shifting half-grown wigglers from incubator pens to their watery slide, bidding adieu to our babies on their way to Sitka Sound, where they will mature and return in two years to complete their life cycle.

Work is a state of mind, an attitude. Ideally, work and play should be compatible, and sometimes they are, but it does take effort. The work world is changing, accommodating flex time, becoming less rigid about family responsibilities and gender roles. All this is good. And with extended life expectancies, there are more opportunities to exercise one's skills. Strive to be mentally alert and continue to maximize levels of energy via physical activity. A choice to volunteer during retirement does all this and, in the process, offers the entire world to investigate. The secret is in the planning.

Pleasures

- First pleasure: Choice of schedule. This may be fixed or flexible; it's up to the individual. After being in Alaska for an entire year, I decided the best schedule for me is to long-distance volunteer for six months and be home for the holidays. A desirable schedule evolves through trial and error.
- Second pleasure: People. Simply associating with those with different attitudes enriches life. Interaction with multi-generational groups may lead you to a fresh point of view. Diverting from the usual routine, readjusting waking and sleeping patterns, energizes and stimulates. All this is excellent physical and emotional activity. Change, even something as minute as switching from the right to left hand or vice versa once-a-week for simple tasks is beneficial. Balance, activity, and a healthy diet improves attitude.
- Third pleasure: Knowledge. The decision to pursue a volunteer retirement lifestyle requires investigation. Computers are not mandatory. You can use one for free at most libraries. With a library card, the world is open to you. Libraries offer the world in a building. Get the picture? Visit. Enjoy. Utilize. Access the Internet, which could be described as

learning while developing eye-hand coordination and exercising the brain. A new lifestyle is stimulating, beneficial, and healthy! A little knowledge is a good thing. Lots of knowledge is amazing.

• Fourth pleasure: And probably the most important—is TIME. Ahhhh... time, that elusive treasure. Time to cultivate gratitude. Time to accomplish some of those things you've always thought about but never been able to realize.

Nurturing friendships is a gentle science. As mentioned, most men do not tend to cultivate friendships and because of that may feel more alone as they age. However, women tend to preserve, encourage, and support friendships on a daily basis by sharing, laughing, and crying.

Circles of friends are invaluable gifts. The strength of a friendship, even a long-distance one, is food for the soul. Friendships sit lightly on the heart. Be appreciative. Express gratitude for shared experiences. Gratitude is an integral part of life. When the "wandering" phase of life is over, if the effort has been made to cultivate friends and friendships, you will reap a reservoir of passion and compassion.

**What comes naturally at Heifer .... ** *"But, where does it come from?" asks the four-year-old, head tilted, shoulder touching her knee, eyes peering at the underside of a momma goat. "From this bag called the udder," the instructor explains, keeping her fingers around the teats, ready to ease more warm milk into the bucket. "Want to try?" The preschooler pops up, grinning, "Yes!"*

The group gathers around, anxious to touch, to squeeze, to experience first-hand where milk comes from before it enters the world of homogenization and refrigeration. That little girl may not fully comprehend her experience, may not associate the milk with hunger and poverty, but this is the Heifer way— teaching awareness squirt-by-squirt, combining the emotional with activities that focus on educating visitors, every day, in every way.

Such was my experience volunteering at the Heifer Learning Center Ranch in the town of Perryville, Arkansas where I learned to appreciate the organic, natural way of growing, processing, and recycling food and waste products. Each day while answering the phone for the Ranch, I listened to newborn lambs bleat; watched staff oversee volunteers as they taught the intricacies of poverty-

ridden communities; witnessed how knowledge and interaction can change the dilemma of hunger. At lunch, I savored the results of carefully tended livestock and gardens deliciously transformed into barbecued chicken, berry cobbler, fresh greens, tomatoes and carrots.

When I wasn't at work I was exploring the Buffalo River, hiking "turtle rocks" at Petit Jean State Park, dipping my fingers into the healing waters at Hot Springs, finding crystals on a switch-back trail, enjoying panoramic views of Arkansas. Such are the simple pleasures of volunteering.

Retirement means having the choice to take time to acknowledge, breathe, and appreciate. Now that all those unplanned retirement hours stretch into the future, make time to prioritize. Working meant charting a course to get children where they needed to be at the appointed time, scheduling appointments in-between, grabbing a few minutes to pick up groceries. In retirement most meals come from a leisurely stop at the supermarket salad bar.

Over the last twenty years, I have noticed a positive shift regarding family responsibility. Both parents work, but employers are more flexible and parents share parenting. In the past, the majority of errands fell to the mother/wife. I truly believe the next generations will concentrate on sharing rather than assigned gender tasks.

Now that retirement is here, the craziness to serve another's needs is less desirable. The most wonderful part of retirement is being able to create a schedule based on your own desires. One of the incentives to retire is the desire not to be held to another's schedule. Now there is time to walk, not run, through the grocery store; to arrive at an appointment on time; maybe even read a book while waiting. There may even be time to detour for an unanticipated stop, just 'because'.

Simple pleasures ...

- *Unscheduled time.*
- *Diamond stars in an onyx sky after sunset in Zion National Park.*
- *Caribou crossing an intersection in Jasper, British Columbia, Canada.*
- *Hazy peach sunrise over Skyline Drive, Shenandoah National Park.*
- *A moment to smile for no reason at all.*

There are many ways to plan a road trip. Some prefer to get in the car and go. As a solo driver, my preference is to access the Internet for information and location. It eliminates guesswork and allows time for sightseeing and hiking. Search maps, look for alternate routes, become acquainted with geology, history and culture—the Internet never sleeps.

After a year in Alaska, I chose a Pacific coast route home. Driving south into Seattle and beyond, I hiked Crater Lake and Yosemite along the way, visiting with family and friends; managed to visit twelve National Parks. It is amazing what a little planning can do.

Free time is a luxury. Decelerate to observe the contours in a cloud formation. Stop to feel the spray of a waterfall, or linger to gaze at the mountain in the distance simply because 'it's there.' This is how we learn how to enjoy every aspect of unscheduled time.

Be forewarned that it does take a while to become accustomed to not rushing from place to place. Allow the pleasure of traveling slowly to wherever your dreams take you, accommodating both the expected and unexpected.

I love planning unique gifts for my grandchildren. When thinking about my Alaska trip, I decided to incorporate a birthday surprise for my granddaughter. I would invite her to serve as navigator on the first leg of the trip. We left from Albany, NY, headed west to Niagara Falls, south to Indiana Dunes National Monument, west again to cross the Mississippi at Rock City, Iowa, and on to an airboat ride on the Platt River at Freemont, Nebraska, before making the ten-hour sprint into Denver. After a few days in Denver, she flew to Kentucky to meet her parents, and I continued on to Alaska, solo. Having her along was a pleasure and a lifetime memory for both of us.

Taking time to plan allows for this type of arrangement. It's when travel must fit into parameters that obstacles are encountered and costs begin to rise. Last minute plans are expensive. Early departures avoid traffic and allow the pleasure of seeing the sunrise. It is also important to get a good night's sleep by ending your drive before dinner.

*"In solitude we give passionate
attention to our lives,
to our memories,
to the details around us."
-Virginia Woolf*

Driving solo, I planned between four to five hours a day on-the-road, enough to get in some serious miles, while leaving time for discovery.

Because I did not realize the convenience and economy of hostels, the amount of money spent on accommodations was considerable. Also, in 2005, gas was more expensive in Canada, probably comparable to today's prices. On the return trip, thanks to encouragement from a fellow volunteer, I stayed at hostels, which substantially reduced expenses.

Solo travel is not without anxious moments. Keep your cell phone charged, maps handy, and tuck a flashlight into the glove box. Stay focused on the task at hand since there is no one for backup. When my driver's side window malfunctioned, forcing an unexpected detour to find a Chevy dealer, I utilized my maps and cell phone and was directed to Calgary where the repair was completed. Also, since Calgary is a large city, I spotted one of my authorized ATM's there.

Good deal!

Simple pleasures .... *Walking the narrow, pebbly path on the outskirts of Jasper, Alberta, Canada, I marveled at the steep sides of the fern-laden Maligne Canyon, barely able to glimpse the thread of river far below. Glancing into a small meadow, I noticed a woman and her dog enjoying a late afternoon picnic. The dog ran over, the woman beckoned. We shared wine, cheese and experiences. What a lovely simple pleasure.*

One of my life's goals has been to visit as many National Parks as possible and I've visited quite a few. My personal criteria for visiting each park include an overnight and at least one hike. It would not be much of an adventure to drive in, take a look, and drive out.

Although some are familiar with the parks listed below, here is some insight to aid others:

- Totem National Park, Sitka: allows up-close viewing of totems and wild-life. Take notice of bear warnings especially during salmon and blue-berry season. A perfect place to observe salmon spawning and watch eagles teach their young to hunt in secluded coves.
- Lewis & Clark National Park (formerly Lewis and Clark National Historical Park), straddles Oregon and Washington and offers breath-taking costal views. The nearby Columbia River Bridge is four miles long. The park offers a trail which allows a walk in Lewis & Clark's footsteps to the sea.
- Crater Lake, Oregon: One of the most inspirational places to meditate. The solitude of an early morning spent gazing into that mysterious cal-dron is something I will never forget.
- Seminole Indian Reservation, Southern Florida: Spent an overnight in a Chickee (grass hut) situated on a marsh. In the early morning, alligators splashed and birds squawked. The museum is a gem.
- Cherokee Heritage Center, Talequah, Oklahoma: Recommended by a fellow volunteer, this unique Indian settlement, established in 1963, pre-serves and promotes Cherokee history and culture. I viewed the Trail of Tears exhibit and strolled through two Cherokee villages, one reminis-cent of the reconstructed colonial village in Sturbridge, Massachusetts. It it a remarkable place.
- Yosemite, California: Yosemite deserves special mention for rocks whose shape and magnitude (I feel) are 'Rubenesque'.

Alligators and inter-cultural camaraderie in the Everglades ....
"Shhhhh . . ." our guide cautions. We stop in mid-step and peek through bare branches to watch a red-tailed hawk swoop down with talons poised to pluck a rodent for breakfast. Cameras click, and we slosh on, water shoes protecting our feet from prolific Mangrove tree roots. "Don't worry about snakes," he whispers, "it's too cold." It doesn't feel cold, I think, wading through ankle deep murky water on the first leg of our Everglade experience, but perhaps I am too enthralled to notice. The young Korean woman in front of me turns and winks. I smile and shrug. An opportunity to slog, hike, and canoe through the Everglades does not come along every day.

Volunteering in Florida offered the opportunity to check out orchids, attend a Seminole Reservation Rodeo, taste swamp cabbage, and explore the Everglades National Park. Again, we hear, "Shhhh." Treading cautiously, we listen. Directly ahead is a tiny pond where momma alligator tends to her babies, a place known to few but our guide. He signals, pointing to the left. A silent approach is impossible. A scurry of splashes is followed by quiet. "Too noisy," he says. We laugh. "No matter," our guide counters, "we'll see some later on."

We see not only alligators but also crocs, Anhinga and two pink spoonbills, close enough to photograph without a telephoto lens. We hike what is termed the "Serengeti of the South" before stopping or lunch.

The afternoon offers a plethora of wildlife and flora, along with socializing with our multigenerational, multi-cultural group. Soon it is time to canoe back. Tired, hungry, and grateful for this abundance of nature, we dip our paddles into red-hued water reflecting the sunset glow and glide past dozing alligators, anxious to partake in the communal meal waiting for us at the hostel in Homestead. After dinner, we relax around a glowing campfire, content, savoring the memory of the day's simple pleasures.

The lesson here is to make time for treasure and pleasure. Partake with leisure but don't overdo. Stay within your own comfort zone, even if you're with people who have more stamina. Preserve and reserve your energy in preparation for the expected and unexpected. Take the climate and your own physical limits into consideration. Be prudent. Do not make yourself vulnerable to a medical emergency which will spoil a wonderful volunteer or travel experience.

While it may be that most of those reading this book are entering the senior years, some of those interested in an alternative lifestyle may not yet be fifty and may be thinking that this does not pertain to them. Not so. It is vital, while living in the present, to plan ahead. File ideas away for future reference. That retiree out there having fun just might know something that may be of value to you. It is obvious that most of us do not learn from history, but maybe, with a little forethought, some will.

This unique lifestyle is also available to college students, recent graduates, and those interrupting their education for whatever reason. At Heifer, students worked, receiving free room and board, thus being independent and "not having to live with Mom & Dad". While email/snail mailing resumes to prospective employers, each student added valuable volunteer skills to that resume.

Also, the unemployed might investigate this option. One thirty-something came up to me in Albuquerque saying, "I have been unemployed for over a year. Buying this book is an investment in myself. Maybe while volunteering, I will find a job!" I hope he did.

Enjoy simple pleasures and ... dream BIG!

Frequently Asked Questions

*1. **Travel is expensive. Gas, food, hotels, a souvenir here or there. It all costs money that I do not have. How do you get around that?** You can cut corners by staying in hostels, eating in and less - two meals a day instead of three. Souvenirs? Just dust catchers. Settle for a bookmark or mail a postcard to family or friends.*

*2. **What about accidents and illness?** Be prepared. Keep a copy of your Advance Directives (Chapter 7) and your insurance information in the car. Utilize resources and volunteer coordinators, fellow volunteers, and insurance personnel. Respond, don't react.*

*3. **I have responsibilities at home and cannot take a lot of time away. How can I volunteer somewhere with so little time to spare?** Offer to volunteer for as little as a month. Travel by train or bus, a longer journey but a simple way to enjoy some time away – a respite. A shorter volunteer span can offer an inexpensive way to take a breather, to read, be along, or experience a totally different environment. Call or email to discuss short-term options with any volunteer coordinator.*

Interview: Leona and Jim

Russell Cave National Monument, Bridgeport, AL

Leona ... *mother, teacher, organizer, Volunteer Experience Workshop Leader and volunteer.*

Jim ... *shipper/receiver, father, Tool Use skills Workshop Leader and volunteer.*

"Our youth leaders had the foresight to write a synopsis of our volunteering experiences," Leona said, "so we have a book of memories which turned into a work-camping booklet and workshop to share with others who are contemplating giving Work-camping a try. This is how, whenever asked," she smiled, "we can explain how to share time and talents through volunteering."

Making a memory book seems like a foregone conclusion, something every volunteer does, but it is not so. As with any vacation or volunteer destination, a written account often is overshadowed by the enjoyment of the moment.

Why Leona volunteers .... *"Oh my, you are asking about a lifestyle!"* she laughed. *"It's what we do. We had a youth minister who started our church* on the path of mission work. It's become a part of who we (as a couple) are. It is giving a hand-up, not just a hand out."

Encouraged and inspired by a hero and heroine who were missionaries in South America for thirty-two years, Jim and Leona divide their volunteer time between home and abroad. Their hands-on-culture seeped teaching, sharing skills and dispelling fears about where to go and what to do takes them to varied destinations across the United States and back.

Why Jim volunteers .... *"It's simple. God commands us to do His work." Jim spoke with genteel confidence. "We see a need and instinct follows. We've been doing it for twenty-five years... it is part of who we are. It just happens."*

As a couple, Jim and Leona have contributed their volunteer efforts for disaster relief, organized work camps, and served meals at their local homeless shelter. Their travels have taken them to Washington, D.C, the Appalachian South Folklife Center in West Virginia, Lani Kamaha'o Peace Village, Hawaii, and H.O.M.E. Inc., in Maine— lots of miles, friendships, and hard work! Also included on their list is jury duty. Many forget that serving on a jury, although required by law, is a form of civic volunteering, just like recycling.

While raising their daughter in the hills of Pennsylvania, Leona enjoyed a career as a public school teacher. "Being organized," she said, "is my salvation. By organizing our efforts, locales and responsibilities, we can contribute more without becoming exhausted with the details. Yes, it is work, and sometimes upsetting to witness the poverty or destruction, but when we have the opportunity to converse with residents, they are anxious to share their stories and are grateful for our help."

As a former shipper and receiver in a manufacturing plant, Jim explained how his work skills easily converted to a volunteer lifestyle. "For those of us who remember, the assembly line required human hands to sort and build." Jim paused to smile, "although currently, most of this type of function has been absorbed by robot arms."

How Jim and Leona organized their volunteer workshops and "carry-along" folder to teach others about work-camping:

- *Carved out a space of time to transfer all information out of our "heads" onto paper;*
- *Organized our experiences into logical form i.e. location, duties and responsibilities of adults vs. adolescents, meals, sleeping arrangements, shared social activities;*
- *Utilized a 3-hole binder with adequate copies, plus saving the information into PowerPoint PC, enabling a presentation with digital pictures;*
- *Distribute binders and/or offer a DVD to interested parties when invited to speak or asked to share information;*
- *Asked participants for feedback and requested others to share stories of responsibilities, faith growth, and/or experiences with others to encourage greater participation.*

We discussed the fact that many repetitive processes have evolved into digital technology, relieving workers from performing tedious, repetitive tasks. "Some think assembly work was tedious but every day was different, some part of the line would bog down and other times we'd have to wait for parts. It teaches you patience, dexterity and offers a sense of accomplishment that you are one part of a whole, not unlike our volunteering. And," Jim added, "We meet so many people as we travel. We are always busy—the word tedious never comes to mind."

As I have stated, my preference is for volunteer assignments which offer free room and board, but Jim and Leona have chosen to volunteer for shorter periods while paying transportation and housing costs themselves. They attempt to stay with friends, or search out inexpensive lodgings for privacy. If this type of volunteer service appeals to you, be certain to check into issues of privacy, personal comfort amenities, and cost(s) before agreeing to volunteer for an extended period of time.

As a volunteer and an author, I have also discovered that the concept of volunteering is ingrained in all who participate, sharing the passion, compassion and skills wherever and whenever. Those who have been sheltered from life's adversity may not have the ability to fully comprehend that circumstances beyond a person's control might have contributed to their plight. Most volunteers do not judge.

When I inquired about experiences abroad, Leona stated, "In 2000, we spent two weeks in Mercedes Octopecki, Honduras, helping to build the local library. I spoke little Spanish and Jim knew one word—'agua'," she laughed. "It was a challenge. Yet Jim and Eldar (a member of the community) worked together to build a wall completely by hand. Many people question why we would want to put ourselves into a situation where there is a language barrier. It is simple... the rewards far outweigh the difficulties. We often think that we are the 'givers' and 'they' are the recipients. But, in the final analysis, we receive so much more than we give. It becomes life changing.

Leona explained that before they traveled to Honduras, the company Jim worked for had donated a fully equipped medical kit—blood pressure cuff, scalpel, clamps, bandages, splints—all they would need, since they would be in the mountains away from medical care other than the local clinic staffed by an intern.

What We Have Learned While Volunteering

- *By rebuilding a home you will have learned learn how to put up dry wall, tape, "mud", sand and prime walls.*
- *The reward of working with those less fortunate is insight, patience, and gratitude.*
- *While every volunteer experience may not be pleasurable, all are applicable to daily life*

In Honduras, all future doctors must serve at least one year in a village clinic. When they left the village, Leona and Jim donated the kit and all the over-the-counter medications and supplies, plus anything else they could come up with by searching their luggage. They even canvassed their travel companions for donations!

Leona and Jim have found that volunteering has given them *pleasure beyond measure*. One cultural experience involving camaraderie in Honduras was mentioned: "The women actually pointed out to their husbands," Leona stated, "that, unlike the local groups, the girls and women in our group worked right beside the boys and men.

The next day the women came to work with us in their dresses and high heels and asked for a meeting where they could learn about women's rights in the United States." When the meeting ran longer than expected, Leona noticed the husbands stood right outside the door, annoyed, waiting for their evening meal.

"The women ignored them," she laughed, "saying (to me) that they would blame the lateness on us, telling their husbands... 'these gringas asked so many questions that we just had to be polite and answer them!' When we left, I kept imagining headlines about an international incident, but guess the men accepted their explanation. We made a small difference without planning to do so. Being a foil for the women was the least we could do."

Another experience was at a homeless shelter when Jim and Leona introduced some adolescents to a new environment. "The high school students we brought along ended up huddled in a corner in tears," Leona said. "They could not understand why this would happen to people—why they would be left without anyone caring about them or without even the basics of life!"

It might be prudent to remember that volunteering is not for the faint of heart. Volunteers offer compassion not criticism, serving without financial compensation and perhaps material comforts. As this gracious couple says, "If the 'why' comes up, you have missed the point".

Leona related the following story about the rewards that come to those who volunteer: "On a mission trip in California, I dropped two young girls off at a center where the homeless receive breakfast. While driving there, I had gone through the basic dos and don'ts, reviewing safety. The girls appeared comfortable, but when I went to leave, they panicked, clinging to each other, needing assurance. I was hesitant, questioning whether I should go or stay but decided to go. It was about eight in the morning. When I returned to pick them up, I could not find them anywhere! Then I heard laughter coming from a nearby building."

Sitting back in her chair, Leona continued. "Well, I headed toward the laughter and found the girls were conversing and joking with the clients. They were not ready to leave and I was pleased they had overcome their fears. Today, one of the women is a medical practitioner delivering babies; the other a minister. While I would not in any way take credit for their careers,

I will continue to hope that like experiences influence the future of any adolescent or adult involved in volunteering."

This couple intends to continue their volunteer efforts wherever there is a need for as long as they are able. I think they will be busy for years to come.

Leona and Jim's active participation in the five stages of retirement.

1. **Imagination**—*Volunteering to chaperone while still in the workplace as an unexpected prelude to a volunteer retirement lifestyle;*
2. **Anticipation**—*Enjoyment of sharing skills and compassion while traveling and meeting new friends ;*
3. **Liberation**—*Dual retirement in 2001;*
4. **Transition**—*Expansion of local and long distance volunteering into organized workshops to teach and encourage others;*
5. **Reconciliation**—*Continuing a volunteer retirement lifestyle, sharing, teaching, enjoying.*

SEVEN:
Heed Needs

"What is it you plan to do with your one wild, precious life."
-Mary Oliver, poet

Healthcare is a dilemma. It's no wonder that health issues, rather than money, are the main focus for our aging public. According to the National Institute of Health, people in the United States are living longer than ever before. Many mature adult live active and healthy lives, but as the years accumulate the body and mind age.

The steps for maintaining a healthy lifestyle are widely publicized, particularly for the over-sixty crowd. They include: eating a balanced diet, keeping active, not smoking, scheduling regular checkups, and awareness for safety at home or away.

We are greeted daily with news of rising health care costs. The good news is that, as our population ages, many are living active, healthy, and productive lives. On average a woman can expect to live to age 84, a man to age 78.

How will we use these extra years? Many people of retirement age choose to continue working. Others travel or spend time with family and friends. Many are volunteering. Lifestyle plays an active role in preventative medicine. If you want to remain healthy and active in the years to come, heed medical, psychological, and spiritual advice.

Rules for a Healthy Life .... *Shouting is rarely heard. Be the last to raise your voice. Most times, shouting indicates loss of control. Shouting is emotional blackmail. People respond to calm.*

By the way, the longest documented human life span is 122 years! New research suggests that young people who assume that life is rough for seniors are more likely to suffer from heart attack and stroke when they reach that age themselves. The findings do not claim that negative assumptions about aging will cause young people to develop cardiovascular problems later, but clearly there is a link. If I am going to be a role model, I choose to be a healthy one.

"It's unlikely that simply thinking happy thoughts about aging will make people live happily ever after, Randy Dotinga says, "but when you see healthy older relatives, you're likely to develop a positive view of aging."[4]

Being mentally healthy and happy while aging is something everyone deserves. Society is mistaken in the belief that aging brings medical and psychological difficulties to all seniors or mature adults.

A healthy lifestyle does not mean treadmills and salads every day, although it's not a bad idea. A healthy activity can be anything from eating an apple to climbing a mountain. It is the degree of difficulty, quality and quantity that counts. Start with these:

Healthy, Smart—and Fun—at Any Age

- **Eat dark chocolate.** Besides being delicious, dark chocolate contains beneficial antioxidants, may lower blood pressure, and provides an energy boost. FACT: chocolate is a fruit. Of course, I am being facetious, but the cacao nut is the fruit of the cacao tree, so having a chocolate milk shake for breakfast offers calcium and fruit. Can you tell me a better way to start the day?
- **Drink red wine**. Red wine is packed with antioxidants which work to protect against the effects of aging. One glass per day is sufficient.
- **Smile**. Smiling is a great way to change an attitude, connect with people, and counteract the effects of stress. By smiling, we "trick" our body into believing that everything is good. Think of smiling as a light switch to change a less-than-positive mood. Try it! FYI—frowning causes deeper wrinkles.
- **Have more sex**, yes... really. Besides being fun and good exercise, sex and touching are essential to good health. Sex releases an assortment

---

4   Healthday: Views on Old Age May Become Reality Later, by Randy Dotinga, February 27, 2009

of beneficial chemicals into the body. Touching emphasizes bonding, strengthens relationships, and increases our own self-worth.

- **Relax**. Relaxation is the opposite of stress. It counteracts harmful health effects and allows our bodies to heal and function better. Practice daily relaxation techniques such as yoga and gentle stretching. Work to turn off stress, replacing it with calm energy to improve blood pressure, heart rate, and the ability to cope with everyday challenges.
- **Make exercise play**. Games and sports are a great way to keep the body and mind healthy. Simple exercises maintain balance, flexibility, endurance and strength. Take a yoga class. Participate in group games such as bowling, tennis. Try Wii, the virtual DVD interactive game. Practice some kind of aerobic exercise or weight training at least three times a week. To maintain good balance, put your socks on standing up! Try board games, puzzles and cards.
- **Sleep**. Some would think this is a no-brainer however sleep is an essential bodily function that is often underrated. Most of us do not get enough. Naps can be beneficial. Catch a fifteen minute snooze at midday. The health benefits of sleep include more energy, a better immune system, and a more pleasant disposition.
- **Spend time with loved ones**. Relationships are an important part of health. Strong bonds build trust and positive interaction that offer protection against depression. Cultivate relationships with family and friends to improve health and life.
- **Be positive**. It is a fact that negativity ages a person. The aging process cannot be controlled, but it can be managed. Let go. Embrace a healthy lifestyle. Search out ways to take pleasure while aging. Enjoy greater learning experiences. Do not whine and whimper over what you cannot control.

Wellness, like life, is not a spectator sport. Each individual is in charge of his or her own personal wellness. We make our own happiness, peace of mind, enjoyment, and satisfaction.

Having a support system to rely on takes effort. For motivation, ask someone to meet you for a morning walk around the neighborhood or join a health club with a friend on a two-for-one membership. Silver Sneakers, a 65-

plus exercise program provided by some health plans, offers free health club membership. Because Silver Sneakers programs are available nationwide through my health plan, I am able to exercise wherever I volunteer, without cost. I advocate Silver Sneakers programs as the best preventative medicine program for seniors. Check with your supplemental plan carrier.

As an alternative to the expense of a gym, visit a Senior Center for information about exercise classes. Parks and Recreation Programs in towns and cities offer low cost exercise programs. Libraries offer resources which connect seniors with exercise programs. As we age, life whirls by faster. When the unexpected happens, meet it with patience and a sense of humor.

My own lifestyle combines enjoying family and friends, volunteering, exercise, yoga, social events and writing. Whenever possible I walk, since I consider walking to be "meditation in motion." I try to live my life without judgment, responsible for myself with compassion toward others, reminding myself not to take things personally.

Rules for a Healthy Life ....
Do not be afraid to dream.
Dreams are limitless.
Dreams are private.
Dreams do not cost money.
Dreams can be improbable.
Dreams can be outrageous.
Dreams are also possible.

I do look to tomorrow by practicing a healthy lifestyle and plan somewhat, but the reality is that there is only today. I truly do try to live every day as if it were my last. This is not negativity, rather a realistic way of reducing procrastination, showing gratitude, and appreciating the moment.

Planning is a healthy action. Planning reduces stress: appointments are kept, train connections are met, car maintenance is appropriate. One major benefit of planning is lower cost. Many types of transportation offer discounts on advance ticket sales—check when you make your reservations. Save money by ordering prescriptions by mail; carpool when possible; when running errands, make right hand turns going and left-hand turns returning.

Rules for a Healthy Life .... *Maintain a healthy brain. Practice preventative medicine. Health is for the entire body, not just from the neck down. Be aware of numbers: body weight, blood pressure, blood sugar levels and cholesterol. Eat less fat and more antioxidant-rich foods. Work the body with physical exercise.*

Search out activities that are fun, like a massage, pedicure, or movie. If this is financially impossible, request a gift card for holidays or birthdays. Attend a lecture, idle away an hour at a bookstore—they expect people to dawdle; that's why the comfy chairs.

If isolation is an issue, or illness and stress become a problem, contact your doctor. Unload on a friend. Just remember, after the crisis passes, be prepared to do the same for that friend. Life is a series of circumstances inside a network of caring people. Enjoy, appreciate—show gratitude. At the back of this book are lists of websites for volunteering and senior issues. Three that specifically pertain to health and aging issues are:

AARP www.aarp.org *;*

National Elder Law Foundation www.nelf.org

National Council on Aging www.ncoa.org.

While researching, I came across an anti-aging quiz initiated by the Mayo Clinic. It is entitled "Secrets to a Longer, Healthier Life." No peeking at the answers that follow:

Mayo Clinic Anti-Aging Quiz *(Answer true or false.)*

1. As long as your body is physically healthy, you'll lead a long and healthy life.

2. Losing weight without even trying is a good thing.

3. As you get older you should reduce the amount of exercise you do each week since you're more likely to hurt yourself.

4. No matter how much you exercise and how healthy your diet, whether you end up sickly or healthy in your later years is largely determined by your genes.

5. As you get older, your body requires less sleep.

6. By the time you reach retirement age, it's too late to erase the effects of a lifetime of bad health habits.

7. Herbal products advertised as anti-aging are a good bet for longer life.

8. Napping during the day is a sure sign of declining health and should be avoided.

9. If you never had any serious illnesses as a young adult, you probably do not have to worry about any serious health problems as you get older.

10. Volunteering in your community is just as good for you as it is for the people you are helping.

No surprise, all answers but one are false. Number ten is true, but that should be obvious. Volunteering within the community is just as good for the volunteer as it is for the community. Volunteering is good for the heart, soul, community, and world.

More Rules for a Healthy Life *............ Enjoy a secret release. Do something simply for the pleasure it gives. Paint a picture. Play the piano. Walk the dog. Ride a bike. Schedule a pedicure. Sing a song. Reorganize a closet. Do nothing while enjoying a quiet moment or two, and bask in the pleasure.*

A positive medical philosophy is important. Because of increased emphasis on good health in our society, even fast food restaurants are reducing fat and salt in food preparation. Maintain a healthy attitude toward diet. There are many important components of retirement, and one of the most important for those sixty-five or older is health coverage through the Medicare program. In addition to Medicare, I feel every senior should be enrolled in a supplemental medical plan, plus prescription drug insurance.

If you are confused by this issue, visit the experts at any local senior center or look for senior medical seminar notices posted in the local library or in the paper. Check the AARP site on the Internet where information about the regulations for different states is continually updated.

I began the process of applying for Social Security benefits online, and found the site very user-friendly. When approaching your perceived retirement age, you can begin this process at www.socialsecurity.gov. Peruse the site for necessary documentation. If you need to pause the process while you do some research you can save all the information entered and return to it at a later time. Visiting a local Social Security office will work, but the online/telephone process is efficient and pleasant.

On a more serious note, we as a population are aging and must plan for death. Travel, even across the street, can be precarious. It is prudent to acquire and preserve important legal documents. Follow these steps for peace of mind:

Protect Important Documents:

- *Gather everything available about income, property, investments, insurance and savings.*
- *Put these important papers and copies of legal documents in ONE place. Put everything in a designated dresser drawer, or simply list the information and location of papers in a notebook. If papers are in a bank safe deposit box, keep copies in a file at home. Put a note on the calendar or computer, and each year check to see if updates are necessary, or if documents need to be amended. For the sake of simplicity, the best option is to set up a "red file" which will be obvious to the person who will oversee your affairs when the time comes. Place all information necessary in this file, and notify only the appropriate person of its location.*
- *Tell a trusted family member or friend where important papers are stored. You need not share personal issues, but someone should know where the information is in case of emergency. If trust is an issue, contact an attorney.*
- *Give consent to attorneys and doctors to speak with caregivers. When questions arise regarding medical or burial issues, an attorney or caregiver may not be able to obtain the necessary information without permission. Give permission in advance to Medicare, credit card companies, banks, and doctors. Check if consent can be given over the phone or if a signature form is necessary. There are many different legal documents that can help you in planning how your affairs should be handled. Many of them are similar, so be certain to obtain the appropriate ones. Also, state laws vary; check with an attorney or a financial planner about state vs. federal laws. Every local library and Senior Center has help available for senior legal issues, and many provide yearly seminars. (See Appendix 2 for information on Important Legal Documents and Power of Attorney.*

In New York (my home state), the Bar Association Elder Law Section provides a wallet-sized Health Care Proxy information card. It also offers a concise "My Annual Legal Checklist" form, a brief outline of what financial and legal forms are on file. This is a handy reminder. Check with a local Senior Services Director or your local state Bar Association.

If you are paranoid, as I am, about do-not-resuscitate directives and wish to obtain a bracelet or necklace emblem, go online for ordering. It may be necessary to order through your state's Department of Health. Google <u>www. dohny.gov</u>. It is advisable to keep this information handy in a wallet or in the car while traveling. You may also contact your doctor, but be prepared that you may be told "no", that some physicians frown on giving a DNR bracelet to someone who does not have serious health issues.

There are varied opinions on what is an important paper. See Appendix 2 for a listing of some items to consider. Remember, with pets, be sure to include the name, address and phone number of a veterinarian.

Regarding Power of Attorney: due to the difficult terminology and subtle differences of each form, it is important to speak with an attorney about obtaining a general Power of Attorney, durable Power of Attorney, joint account, trust, or Advance Directive. Though documents may appear alike and have similar titles, each is suited to a particular circumstance.

Rules for a Healthy Life .... *Give the gift of freedom by letting go of children and material goods. Create life as it happens. Control is a burden.*

When visiting any attorney, ask about fees prior to scheduling an appointment. If paying the costs of an attorney will be difficult on your budget, visit the local Senior Center to ask for a referral, or confide in a trusted family member to help manage some of these issues. Having our affairs in order is comforting. It frees us to get on with the business of living our lives. Many documents pertaining to wills, Advanced Directives, and Power(s) of Attorney are available online for free. Be certain to research thoroughly.

If you decide to serve with an organization based outside the U.S., take the precaution of investigating how to deal with an emergency abroad. Go to <u>www.travel.state.gov/traveltips.com</u> for information on dealing with situations such as: lost or stolen passports, a medical or general emergency, what to do in case of the death of a U.S. citizen traveling abroad, transferring money, quarantine and customs regulations, and many other issues.

Keep in mind that an assignment abroad may be within an unstable political environment. In researching the Internet, I found that the Department of State and U.S. embassies and consulates will provide assistance to all U.S. citizens abroad if needed. However it is up to the individual volunteer to investigate the status of a destination country. Broadcast services like the BBC give insight to status. Volunteering abroad is a fantastic experience. Take precautions. Be savvy about your travel.

A Few more rules for a Healthy Life … Embrace good ethics. Do a good job. Be kind. Be honest. Understand the politics of life. This does not mean submission, it means acceptance. A kind heart is a healthy heart.

Of course, one rule of a volunteer retirement lifestyle, whether volunteering at home or abroad is to keep a journal. It can be as simple as a log-book-type with dates, places and personal information for networking purposes, or as elaborate as a record of your daily thoughts and actions. It is amazing how often I refer to names and address, snail-or e-mail, during the course of a week. The world becomes more manageable when friends are but an e-mail away

Another rule, perhaps equal with the first, *is to enjoy.*

Frequently Asked Questions

1. **Why do I need Advanced Directives?** *If you consider that it is not important what happens after your death, you can ignore Advance Directive paperwork. However, if the way that lifesaving devices or feeding tubes, burial, and health care are handled is vital to your peace of mind, it is imperative to make those wishes known. Doctors are schooled to preserve life at all costs; they take an oath. Don't put them or your family in the difficult position of guessing what you want. Put your wishes in writing.*

2. **Why do I need a will—I don't own anything to leave to anyone!** *For the same reason Advance Directives are necessary. List assets and proceed accordingly. Probate is the number one reason for a will. A simple will may be obtained online.*

3. **How about an itinerary for my family?** *I don't need mine to know every move I make, do I? Family members are interested in your safety and well-being.*

Just because they ask to know your destination or the route you choose does not mean they are prying. Give them numbers along your route. Once you have arrived at a destination, the name and number of the volunteer organization with Volunteer Coordinator's contact information should be sufficient. A cell phone is a handy way to keep in touch. It also gives others who cannot travel a chance to share vicariously in your adventures.

4. ***What about prescription medications while volunteering?*** *This situation came up in Arkansas. Solution? Sign up for mail delivery. Speak with someone at the post office for a temporary address change and don't forget to change it back on your return. Mail order prescriptions are also more economical.*

5. ***Any Miscellaneous tips?*** *I need all the help I can get: When traveling, keep copies of credit card information, driver's license, etc in a separate envelope. Re-applying for lost items is much easier with a copy in hand.*

Interview: Mary

Heifer University Workshop, Perryville, AR

Mary ... *professor and education administrator, Heifer volunteer coordinator, friend, community volunteer and passionate speaker for sustainable causes.*

"On October 16, 2005, I woke up at three in the morning," Mary said, passionate to share her experience. "I knew that I had to retire ... NOW. I knew that what I experienced within the Navajo environment was the calling I had felt for so long," she laughed.

Mary laughs a lot, a hearty laugh engaging all within hearing.

"I got out of bed and started refiguring my finances. I had just signed a three-year contract with the University, great perks and everything, but you must make a break while you can do it with zest and fire in your belly."

Mary spent thirty years in education, changing her focus every six years or so to keep herself challenged. She was Director for Community Service Learning at the University of Texas, Arlington when she made the decision to retire.

"I worked for a visionary president who supported service learning as an integral part of the classroom, relevant to the theoretical content of the course being taught with appropriate reflection at the conclusion. This reflection, an opportunity for each student to examine their life relative to the course taken, enabled each to see how they, as an individual, fit into the larger picture. I, too, utilized this theory in deciding my retirement goals."

It was during her tenure as Director for Community Service Learning that Mary began to investigate Heifer International. She heard about the Heifer Study Tours and wanted to go and learn; to witness the dignity professed first hand, to see if "it was what they said it was." It was. And so began her sojourn.

Mary believes that a person must challenge one's own perspectives instead of staying comfortable. "Comfort is safe," she says, "but it is not growth."

Before pursuing her career in education, Mary considered joining the Peace Corps, but instead, prior to her retirement decision, she volunteered within her Texas community through her church and various local organizations.

She also traveled throughout the United States and the world on the volunteer staff of the U.S. Wheelchair Sports Team. "You really haven't experienced the world of travel until you accompany one-hundred individuals in wheelchairs," Mary said. "It took a great deal of dexterity, patience and perseverance, but they were up to it, more so than I."

Why Mary volunteers .... *"I feel volunteering is a calling, a service learning calling with a spiritual link. It has taken me a long time to define that calling."*

When Mary decided to participate in a Heifer Navajo Study Tour, she took a step back, watching and listening. One of the most enduring lessons garnered from the Navajo is that a community does not solve social problems by money alone through quick fixes and handouts.

Not that this was a huge revelation, but the realization that to reach realistic solutions to hunger and poverty there is a need for collaboration – not confrontation—was. Equally important is giving responsibility back to the people involved along with restoring cultural dignity. This, Mary observed, is the Heifer way and she wanted to participate in this process, but how? – more importantly, how soon?

Texas born and bred, Mary travels her state as a volunteer, living the message of service learning. Throughout her career she held to the belief that students benefit from mentoring, enabling them to search out opportunities, contributing to the common good. She has walked the walk—having mentored and been mentored. Her philosophy is to stay engaged.

"Service learning is so important," Mary said, enthusiastic in her gestures. "Service learning investigates, engages, assesses the need and participates in the solution. You don't go out to fix and walk away. It has nothing to do with education or social status. I learned so much from a poor indigenous woman... it was pretty humbling. Being on the Navajo reservation taught me that only through watching and listening can you truly help. In my retirement I want to apply those skills toward the greater good."

Navajo Nation .... Personal growth is very significant in Navajo tradition. The stages of a person's life are recognized, accepted, and celebrated. A child's first laugh is an important event. A girl's coming of age is marked by kinaaldá, the girl's puberty ceremony. According to Navajo tradition, this celebration lasts four days. Each morning at dawn the girl runs to the east; the last two days are reserved for singing, praying and ritual activities. During the ceremony, relatives and friends stop by to visit the girl's family, bringing food and eating. On the last night, the girl, her family, and the Shaman sit up all night and sing. In the morning she runs to the east for the last time and upon return cuts a corn cake prepared the day before, the heart going to the Shaman. After the ceremony, the girl is ready for marriage.

During the PowerPoint presentation Mary gave at Women's Lambing Week at the Heifer Ranch in Perryville, Arkansas, she directed attention to the screen filled with pictures of various projects and proud smiling faces.

"It is all about the intricacies of how to work within the culture to achieve sustainability. Who is the mentor? Who is the teacher?" she asked of those gathered. "How do you keep the community alive and involved? It is about what you have in common, not what makes you different. I love Heifer because Heifer projects 'are the people'. My goal is to be a voice for those who do not get heard. I went to the Navajo nation and was changed. I cannot let this passion die within. I must do something."

Another volunteer effort of Mary's is the Heifer Garden Project in Dallas. This community garden, serviced by many volunteers and organizations, thrives in one of the poorer sections of Dallas. Elementary and homeschoolers, adolescents and preschoolers come to learn about worm composting, or vermiculture, and how to grow vegetables in a garden which is something many of them do not witness on a daily basis.

Mary and her friend, dressed as MOOEY the cow and CLUCKY the chicken, love to explain the particulars of planting, cultivating and harvesting to the younger groups, the two to four year-olds. They grab the children's attention with cow and chicken hats and proceed to teach them, via conversation and sign language (her friend is a teacher to the deaf), about the joys of gardening.

Using animal puppets, the children are entertained and informed. After the puppet show, the children get to harvest produce for the Food Bank. They pick and weigh, measuring portions, some older groups actually using arithmetic to figure the cost per serving. Mixing math and manure... great concept!

Mary is a woman on a non-stop mission. Her time at the Ranch in Perryville was a brief respite from her busy schedule. Pausing to reflect on what has been accomplished, yet anticipating future initiatives, she said, "The Navajo Study Tour was a transformation in my life. They knew something I had not yet figured out. I learned how the gift of a sheep brings hope, dignity and self-reliance to indigenous people who struggle to preserve their culture, traditions and language."

Mary sighed, reminiscing. "The most substantive lesson was to investigate the intricacies of hozho—harmony within myself, with others and with Mother Earth and Father Sky. Two Navajo words combine to form the equivalent of Ying/Yang: hozho loosely translating to beauty and harmony, and hocho which means disorder. Being on Navajo time helped me rediscover a rhythm, simplicity and harmony long lost, which prompted me to explore and understand my Cherokee heritage."

At the conclusion of Mary's presentation at the Heifer Learning Center there were numerous questions, curiosity about her Navajo experience with the Churro sheep, and amazement at how Mary maintains the stamina and flexibility to garden with the two-year-olds with one hand, while mentoring and raising money with the other.

Navajo Nation .... Churro sheep are considered Navajo sheep, especially among the elders. These sheep are an integral component of Navajo tradition, culture and spirit. The four horns of the Churros represent the four sacred mountains marking the Dinetah, or Navajo homeland.

Churros also come in many colors: creamy white, representing the East, gray, the South; brown-red, the West, and black, the North. Navajo mythology says the sheep are a gift from their creator spirit, Changing Woman, and that Spider Woman, a deity who resides at Spider Rock in nearby Canyon de Chelly, taught the Navajos how to weave.

Humble to a fault, she shrugged. "I want to focus on the difference between volunteering and service learning—the difference in remaining at arm's length and serving in the trenches of humanity," she said. "I would like the world to know that hunger is caused not by a scarcity of food, but a scarcity of democracy. Service without learning leaves us vulnerable to perpetuating the inequities to which we have grown accustomed and failing to become the public problem solvers that the world so needs. During my retirement years, I want to be one of those solvers."

I would say that she is well on her way.

Mary's active participation in the five stages of retirement.

*1. **Imagination**—Mary recognized the possibility of transforming a calling into a quest—holding true to... love the journey, not the destination;*

*2. **Anticipation**—Every six years changed her educational career, preparation for later challenges by instilling the belief that what you do today opens the doors to tomorrow;*

*3. **Liberation**—Mary "woke up at 3:00 a.m. and decided this is it! Life is about choices and knowing that what may be good for my financial security may not be good for my soul";*

*4. **Transition**—She resigned while reconfiguring her financial situation;*

three months later retired. Motto: transition may change your location, but transformation happens when life touches you;

*5. **Reconciliation**—In reflection, Mary went through a year of mourning angst after retiring from a career that defined her. She emerged redefined as a messenger for those individuals whose voices are not heard because of poverty and lack of education and resources, but who are resourceful and committed to moving toward a better life.*

EIGHT:

Use it or Lose it

> *"Cheerfulness and contentment are great beautifiers and are famous preservers of youthful looks."*   Charles Dickens, novelist (1812-1870)

Enjoy your days, enjoy your life. Be creative. Sculpt your body, mind and attitude through mental and physical exercise as a model for others to emulate. Your time on this good earth is short. Make the best of what is offered. A positive attitude results in a positive life.

It is a fact that frowning causes wrinkles, so smile, even in the face of adversity. Yes, these days there is a lot to frown about. However, there is good news! It has been proved that humans are just as capable of learning in the second half of life as in the first. There is a catch—you have to use it or lose it.

From day one, the brain is ready to learn, ready to capture experiences and commit them to memory. As learning progresses from pre-school to death, the actions you take engage the brain in memorization and organization.

However, learning and memory are not the same. Learning is how new information is acquired; memory is how it is stored. Do not blame memory issues on the fact that "poor memory runs in the family!" Experts say that only about 30 percent of physical aging can be traced to our genes; the rest is up to us.

There are steps to take to achieve the maximum benefit from learning:
- Slow down. You assimilate information best when you concentrate and focus.

- Organize thoughts into a logical sequence.
- Write it down!
- Repeat (remember from first grade, "repeat, review, repeat") and visualize to commit a thought to memory.

In this hectic world, rushing is habitual. Busy-ness causes chaos in the brain resulting in irreparable, albeit invisible, wear and tear. Consequently, not all learning lasts in memory. A phone number is remembered just long enough to program it into your cell phone. Why remember? Scroll down and access. Unless the phone is disabled (and even then the data can be restored) the number is there for eternity and beyond. Each individual memorizes and categorizes differently. Each brain is unique in learning and storing what is learned.

The Hereafter

"How've you been?" asks the man, greeting his neighbor. "Not so great," the woman sighs, pausing at her front steps, "I find that lately I've been thinking a lot about the hereafter." "Really?" says the man, frowning, concerned. "Tell me about it." "Well," the woman laughs," every time I walk into a room, I turn around and wonder what I came in here after."

Memory lapses happen at all ages, at twenty as often as at sixty. Memory sometimes is a gauge by which dexterity is judged. What thought comes to mind when an older person has a memory lapse or stumbles?

The truth is that our brain does not change much with aging. Our vocabulary may become more sophisticated, but as learning progresses, the present combines with the past and our history, as it is stored, becomes more complex.

For the brain, long-term memory is a snap. It is short-term memory or those in-between memories, the facts or events seldom accessed, that become blurred.

Now, do not confuse memory and wisdom. Wisdom is a whole other matter. Wisdom, although most associated with elders, is more an accumulation of life experience than age. Some perceive wisdom as an enhanced capacity to grasp the essence of a complex situation and act accordingly. This type of maturity can be there at age twenty as well as ninety.

While aging, endeavor to learn from past mistakes as well as successes, integrating each into the present to be applied to daily challenges. This leads to the advantage of judgment.

Acquired knowledge is kept active by:

- Thinking positive, tuning out negatives.
- Maintaining social networks.
- Managing stress in a positive manner.
- Engaging the brain. Take it off automatic pilot.

Culturally, we tend to overlook the value of tradition. Residing in a communal setting is tied into culture and is widely practiced outside the United States. Currently there is a growing trend to return to this type of living arrangement since it is useful in solving day care issues, for overseeing the care of the elderly, and last but certainly not least, preserving extended families.

The interaction alone is enough to keep mind and body active. Try caring for a two-year-old or memorizing the schedules of adolescents!

Remembering and forgetting are normal happenings in daily life. If instances of forgetfulness become a problem, speak with a physician or with a friend to get another's perspective. Feedback is important. The example of Ed illustrates how volunteering stimulates physical and mental dexterity.

Remaining alert to your own personal physical and psychological status is not selfish. In retirement, utilize T4M. What is T4M? It is taking the time to draw upon inner desires, dreams and goals, in other words, time to make ... *Time 4 Me.*

Ed............ *Ed got his chance to utilize the skills he had developed in the workplace through SmartWorks, a broker for non-profit agencies seeking willing volunteers with appropriate skills to meet essential unfulfilled needs resulting from budgetary or personnel inadequacies. Along with another local volunteer, he was asked to develop, implement, and evaluate a financial literacy program for low-income seniors. The project was funded in part by The United Way of the Greater Capital Region of New York and focused on realistic solutions for seniors choosing to remain in their own homes in the community.*

"To make it easier for the participants, we offered a club atmosphere," Ed

said. *"This format allowed all of us to engage with each other on equal terms during the eight monthly sessions. We called them Dollars and Sense Clubs."*

Ed, raised in a low-income neighborhood of Brooklyn during the 1950's, is familiar with money issues. After graduation from the City University of New York, working for the State of New York made him aware of the war on poverty. "In hindsight," he said, "it became clear to me that this was a wonderful idea, just not smart enough."

His 34-year career with state government gave him another look at the inefficiencies of big organizations from the inside. He pondered the possibility of philanthropic options in retirement. Then along came the opportunity with SmartWorks! When the sessions were over, 40 out of 114 (35%) surveyed stated that they do plan to make changes in their personal finances as a result of attending club meetings. "We felt this was a good, solid result for everyone's effort!" Ed said with a smile, "and we all enjoyed the experience."

Each generation has a code word or phrase that defines the actions and attitude of a given period of time. Progressing from the 1920's there are the Traditionalists, the Boomers, the X'ers and the Generation Y's. Just how did these groups evolve? What part does attitude play? What about ethics?

What's in a Name?
- **Traditionalists**: Born between 1928 and 1945: conservative, emphasize adherence to custom, social order, faith, liberty and tradition; the WWII generation, attitude shaped by many policies and procedures still in place. Catch phrase: "But it's always been done this way." Money stands as a symbol of reward and motivation.
- **Boomers** (have dropped the baby): Born between 1946 and 1964: Came of age in the 1960's and 70's at time of causes and revolutions. Offspring of the keeping-up-with-the-Joneses generation, they were the first group to be specifically targeted by marketers. Sometimes they wonder, "Is this all there is?" This group feels the need to get involved and "change" things. Catch phrase: "Whoever dies with the most toys wins!"
- **Generation X'ers:** Born between 1965 and 1976: "Latchkey" kids, full of independence, resilience and adaptability. Do not need "someone

looking over their shoulder," but at the same time demand immediate feedback. A small group, but most likely to take over current leadership roles, Xers grew up with the Internet. More individual than a team player. Boomers are counting on Xers to keep Social Security going. This group accepts diversity, are pragmatic, self-reliant and individualistic. Most reject rules, mistrust institutions, own a computer, and utilize technology. They multitask, are generally casual, love flexibility and freedom and consider their workplace to be a friendly place to learn. Catch phrase: "Think out of the box."

- **Generation Y**, or Millennials: Born between 1977 and 1998: Just now beginning to enter the workforce. Expected to be the largest consumers. Grew up with instantaneous media violence. Multi-taskers in a worldwide community, they are not stressed by technology, having been plugged into the Internet from birth. However, they may be dismayed by the inefficiency of corporate processes. Money matters; personal time matters more. They acknowledge and celebrate diversity, are optimistic yet realistic, self-inventive and individualistic. They love to rewrite the rules. This group nurtures friends and family. They enjoy relationships, are prepared for demands, and possess high expectations. Catch phrase: "Text me."

Since the Traditionalists are probably retired or are about to enter retirement, among the three remaining groups still working, the Boomers may be the most fortunate. They may actually retire retirement— economic uncertainty means that many are choosing to remain in the workforce. With the shortage of qualified workers, employers may welcome them as consultants. The workplace relationship is in flux.

Some of the questions all the groups are asking are: How do I fit into the new demographics? How do I adapt my skills to an increasingly chaotic and demanding world? How do I attain a level of comfort in a changing workplace environment or adjusting to full-time leisure? And, most importantly, how do I sustain my current lifestyle? These are all good questions, answered only by thoughtful research and planning.

Why Ed volunteers .... *"To do as much as I can for the organizations who aim to right the socioeconomic wrongs I care about and who hold the most promise to maintain significant impact on those wrongs. I will continue this focus during my remaining time on earth."*

Being a Traditionalist, I chose to volunteer in Alaska. Many of my peers were astonished, and some horrified, that I would travel alone to an unfamiliar place to reside with strangers.

However, I had already spent most of my life thinking outside the box. A lifestyle of nomadic independence is difficult to stop once it starts. I went from adventure to another. Some were difficult, some pleasant. This is how I ended up in Alaska. The idea of volunteering in retirement snowballed, gathering speed over time, and ultimately led to my journey to Sitka.

What retirement is all about!
- *Attitude—keep it positive.*
- *Optimism—it's not what happens, but what you make of it.*
- *Relationships—those that work take work.*
- *Physical and psychological—healthy body and mind.*
- *Rationale—encourage and tolerate diversity.*
- *Inventory—every few months ask, "How Am I Doing?"*

Regardless of adjustments in the workplace due to demographics, technology and our aging population, those facing a life expectancy of thirty-plus years after age sixty-five are making revolutionary decisions. This group is entering a new phase of life, a healthy, active non-childrearing period to enjoy, reconfigure, and redesign life according to their abilities, health status, and circumstances. And despite common perceptions about the miseries of old age, psychologists tell us that people actually get happier as they grow older.[5] Yes! Because the brain functions that govern emotional responses may become less reactive to negative stimuli, potential threats are simply not as threatening, and older people, realizing they have less time to waste, begin to focus on human connections that are more satisfying.

5   Loneliness, by John T. Cacioppo and William Patrick, W.W. Norton & Co. 2008, pp. 219

It has been reported that by 2050 there will be enough people over 100 years-of-age in the United States to populate the city of San Francisco. Those born in the 1940's, 1950's, or 1960's are and will continue to transform the nation's financial and cultural landscape. Some major transformations are the aging workforce and the increased numbers of working mothers into that workforce, along with outsourcing, immigration, and globalization. Given the current financial crisis, many Boomers are prepared to "work forever".

Retirement is being redefined and reinvented. Because of access to health care and extended longevity, most will stay in retirement for thirty years. This is extraordinary since most of the parents or grandparents of current retirement

Ed's active participation in the five stages of retirement.

1. **Imagination**—*the realization that now was the time to act on his "yearned for" priorities;*
2. **Anticipation**—*as retirement got closer, Ed remembers being advised not to wait to start trying out new activities. He and his teen-age son signed up as volunteer "friendly home visitors" to an elderly couple. Also, for the first time, he met with a financial planner. In his final weeks of work, he faced a mountain of retirement choices, and discovered SmartWorks in the process;*
3. **Liberation**—*retirement started with a wonderful retirement party. Since Ed chose to retire in the spring, he planted his biggest, best vegetable garden ever, with more time for weeding, composting, harvesting, and at the same time started two Smartworks projects;*
4. **Transition**—*Ed admits, "Life is rarely a bowl of cherries!" After re-tiring he faced both good and bad; parental dementia, a daughter's marriage, college for his wife and son. Still, as a family advocating a volunteer lifestyle, the family agreed to host an exchange student from Mexico. "Luckily," Ed says, "it got heavy at roughly the same time my first SmartWorks projects were concluding. I pushed the pause button until the smoke cleared." Remember that retirement transition is not always smooth;*
5. **Reconciliation**—*as the weeks and difficulties passed, Ed found he could carve out time to focus on the present. He is now enjoying his family, a larger garden and one new volunteer project. In all of his endeavors, Ed is*

determined that any volunteer project he undertakes will address the societal issues he cares most about. His generation never reached what is considered the age of retirement. Life to them was birth, marriage, children, and death. Leaving the world of work was a distant possibility, not reality.

Remain happy! Continue to participate with groups that advocate exercise, diversity and busyness, and the transition into retirement will hardly be noticed. Anticipate is the name of the game. When you reach forty, start to prepare yourself for those extra thirty years.

My personal advice for all retirees today and forever is to make the personal investment to stay fit in mind, body, and spirit. Embark on a social retirement to channel workplace skills into an energizing lifestyle. If you do, remember that a volunteer is a person serving for a stated period of time in a temporary responsibility, someone who will eventually return home or travel elsewhere. The department or person being "helped" has a financial stake within the politics of an organization. Leave control at the doorstep.

Relinquishing control does not mean you should ignore discrepancies or blatant wrongs. It only means that as an outsider, you have the ability to view the situation from a different perspective, that of someone with no responsibility except to the moment. Trust others to remedy long-term issues or problems.

A volunteer should not mix in the internal politics of an organization. When tempted, I often recite silently, "Shut your mouth, Barbara, shut your mouth." Occasionally you may be treated as or thought of as just a volunteer. Get over it, under it, around it. Remember you can leave, which is something a staff person may not be able to do.

The Benefits of Volunteering ....

Volunteers carry the values and traditions of American society outside of business or government. They do not produce a product or enforce regulations; rather they foster self-help and good will.

America's first volunteers were our immigrant ancestors who fought for freedom. The spirit of American volunteerism is compassionate teamwork personified.

Volunteer organizations encourage people to work with a wider group of other individuals toward a common goal, enabling each to learn more about themselves and to approach issues in their unique way.

Volunteering is a cure for boredom, a remedy for feeling unappreciated, a tonic, and an opportunity for adventure and new experiences.

Volunteering teaches that people and situations can be changed through integrity and trust.

The decision to retire is personal. It may involve a partner, but it is still one person's decision. It may be a see-saw, a "can't afford to go and can't afford to stay" situation. Keep your hands, heart and mind occupied in the meantime by volunteering locally. Look for opportunities on the Internet.

Think about the emotional, financial and social aspects of retirement. In the past, choice was nonexistent. Today there is time and a smorgasbord of options, however many people are unprepared. Be ready, willing and able when the opportunity presents itself!

Since my retirement, I've traveled more than I did in my entire life. I deliberately make time to hike, speak with others, and enjoy life. Unlike most retirees, I did not think about retirement until I was sixty-four.

Some say they began planning to retire from the time they began working. Now well into retirement, I feel one year is sufficient when accumulated financial resources are small. Set goals. Attempt to fit dreams into those goals. Weave some of those goals into whatever is happening right now. Then, when life interferes, there will not be the usual what if?

Would I have done anything differently to prepare for retirement? Maybe negotiate a higher salary to save more in preparation for leaner years. But that didn't happen, and so be it. Living lean as I do is not the most secure place to be, but there is Social Security and I do have a small emergency fund. Living within financial constraints is not new to me. It may be an adjustment for others. Some think living on a shoestring is scary and exhausting, even humiliating, but I guess it depends on how tight you tie the laces.

It has been said that a positive attitude along with compassion and exercise equals good health. If so, I must be the healthiest retiree on the planet!

Frequently Asked Questions

1. ***Just retire?*** *It's scary! I am the sort of person who needs that long-range plan. Let go. How do you know how long you have? Age teaches us that the future is precarious at best. Be in the moment with a wink to the future. Thoughts are more easily altered than long-range plans.*

2. ***I am in a cocoon of family, friends, and church. How do I leave that to go off and do something totally new?*** *You don't have to. There are many opportunities just outside your door. Ask some of those friends to join you in volunteering at a library, hospital or school. Whatever you do will serve as an example to others.*

3. ***It sounds like the new social retirement is the best of both worlds—is it?*** *I would say YES!*

APPENDIX 1: FORMS

ORGANIZATION EVALUATION
(Questions to ask when considering a volunteer opportunity):
1. Do I agree with the mission statement, goals/values of the volunteer organization?
Does the organization have a particular political or religious affiliation similar to mine?
I wish to volunteer _____ hours during an 8 hour day.
I wish to work a _____ hour week.
I would rather not work during the holidays; rather spend with family?
_____ yes _____ no

2. Will the skills that I have match with the positions offered?
I would be interested in manual labor? Office work? Outdoors? I would love to do something new? (example: livestock as opposed to teaching)

3. When are volunteers utilized – what months? Are some months more demanding?
Is there training schedule?
I want to be home during _____ time.
I want to be away from the cold and snow.
I must be home for: _____, _____, and _____.

4. Is the organization (or locations offered) in a place where I am comfortable?
Mountains/desert? Abroad? Home? My ideal volunteer position would be:
Right around the corner _____ yes _____ no
Within _____ miles of my home.
A totally different environment? Why?

5. Is the organization willing to give names of past or present volunteers that I can contact?

Name: _____

Phone/email: _____

Name: _____

Phone/email: _____

6. What housing is offered; shared/communal living, single apartment, roommate?

RV hook-ups? _____ yes _____ no

Single apartment: _____ yes _____ no Shared: _____ yes _____ no

7. Are meals offered? Three meals: _____ yes _____ no

Only lunch (I am responsible for others) _____ yes _____ no

I am responsible for meals: _____ yes _____ no

There is a stipend? _____ yes _____ no Amount: $_____

8. Job titles available? Responsibilities? Ask if a packet or letter will be sent to your home address. Be certain it is a match with your ability.

Handbook to be snail mailed _____ e-mailed _____

Contract/Letter of intent mailed _____ e-mailed _____

9. Costs? Fee(s)? _____ yes _____ no

What are they: _____

10. Will I be working as part of a group (as in Habitat for Humanity) or on my own (as a receptionist, maintenance, librarian)? Supervisor?

Will there be training?

I would like on-the-job-training? _____ yes _____no

11. Be certain of the age group involved unless you do not have a preference to work with older, younger, or mixed groups. Ask about age range; male/female ratio, if important. Multigenerational group?

_____ yes _____ no

12. When you have the particulars, review carefully BEFORE you commit. Clarify "volunteer vacation" vs. volunteer commitment. Costs involved are very different.

Resume required? _____ yes _____ no

What I really want to do: _____

NOTES:

SELF-EVALUATION

By answering the questions truthfully, YES OR NO, you will see what you need to do, or at the very least, a clear picture of what to expect—unless some kind of change is not on your horizon:

Am I patient with myself and new opportunities? Yes _____ No _____

Have I nurtured family, friends and acquaintances that will assist in my transition? Yes _____ No _____

Do I have sufficient financial resources for the lifestyle I wish to pursue or will funds be limited? Yes _____ No _____

If I choose to travel within the U.S. or abroad, can I easily adapt to a new culture? Do I suffer from anxiety in new situations? Yes _____ No _____

Have I made a plan for my new life? Yes _____ No _____

Is my self-esteem sufficient to make the transition from working full-time to working part-time, or not at work-place to the leisure of retirement?
Yes _____ No _____

Am I looking forward to new opportunities? Yes _____ No _____

Is my partner looking forward to my retirement? (may not apply)
Yes _____ No _____

Am I able to handle my own medical emergencies? Yes _____ No _____

Is my passport current? Yes _____ No _____

Am I willing to spend the hours necessary to research appropriate opportunities? Yes _____ No _____

Will my family resent my leaving the immediate area? Have I left explicit information regarding health, finances, death and itinerary?
Yes _____ No _____

Am I happy? Yes _____ No _____

FIVE STAGES OF RETIREMENT

Number 1—**IMAGINATION**:
(What is that wish that never happened?)

Number 2—**ANTICIPATION**:
(Will it actually happen? Will I/we make it? Did we plan for all possibilities?)

Number 3—**LIBERATION**:
(I am free! What am I doing?)

Number 4—**TRANSITION**:
(This is wonderful! This is not what I pictured.)

Number 5—**RECONCILIATION**:
(List all of what is hoped; the maximum possibilities.)

APPENDIX 2: DOCUMENTS

EXPLANATION OF TERMS AND DOCUMENTS

Wills and trusts describe how you wish to give away your money and property after you die. A will simply directs how your estate should be distributed. What a will won't do[6]—and what it will is this: it will not dispose of all kinds of property but it will govern some transfers of real estate. It will not keep itself up to date but it also won't let you avoid probate. It will cost less than a trust but won't take effect before you die. It also will not compel good behavior among your heirs but will be more effective if its contents and whereabouts are known. Check with an attorney for matters regarding wills and trusts.

A living will (also called an Advance Directive or Medical Directive) gives you a say in decisions regarding your health care if you are incapacitated. It describes your wishes for your care at the end of your life. Having a living will may well make things easier for family and/or caregivers when it comes time to make decisions on your behalf. Make your wishes known explicitly to the appropriate person.

A general Power of Attorney also allows you to give someone else the authority to act on your behalf, but this power will end if you are unable to make your own decisions.

A durable Power of Attorney allows you to name someone to act on your behalf for any legal task if you are unable to make your own decisions.

A durable Power of Attorney for health care allows you to name another person to make medical decisions for you if you are unable to make them yourself.

---

6   Article on personal finance, What a Will Won't Do (and What it Will), AARP Magazine, Nov/ Dec 2007, Barbara Mlotek Wheiehan, writer

WHAT SHOULD BE CONSIDERED AN IMPORTANT PAPER?
PAPERS:
- Full legal name, date and place of birth
- Social Security number
- Legal residence
- Names and addresses of spouse and children
- Location of birth and death certificates, certificates of marriage, divorce, citizenship, adoption, living will, Advance Directives, Medicare card
- Employers and dates of employment (last employer if retired)
- Medications taken regularly
- Education and military records
- Names and phone numbers of close friends, relatives, lawyer, financial advisor, doctors, religious contacts, memberships in organizations with contact

FINANCIAL RECORDS:
- Sources of income and assets—pension funds, IRAs, 401(k)s, interest, etc.
- Social Security and Medicare information
- Investment information (stocks, bonds, real estate) and stock brokers' names and phone numbers
- Insurance information (life, health, long-term care, home, car) with policy numbers and agents' names and phone numbers
- Bank names with account numbers (checking, savings, credit union) and contact information, including location of safe deposit box and key
- Copy of most recent tax return
- Location of most current will with original signature (most generally left with an attorney –keep a copy)
- Liabilities, including property tax: what is owed to whom, when payments are due, along with mortgages and debts—how and when paid
- Location of original deed of trust for home and car title and registration
- Credit and debit card names and numbers

RESOURCES
(CHECK LOCAL LIBRARIES)

ABC's for Seniors: Ruth Jacobs, Ph.D., Hatala Geroproducts , 2006 and Be an Outrageous Older Woman: Ruth Jacobs, Ph.D., HarperPerennial, 1993 (revised)

Achieving the Good Life After 50: Renée Lee Rosenberg, The Five O'Clock Club, 2007

Aging Nation: The economics and politics of growing older in America; Authors: James H. Schulz and Robert H. Binstock; 2006

Change Your Life Through Travel: Jillian Robinson, Footsteps Media, 2006

Defying Gravity: Prill Boyle, Emmis Books, 2004

Encore: Marc Freedman, Public Affairs, member of Perseus Books Group, 2007

Fountain of Age: Betty Friedan, Simon & Schuster, 1993

Ground of Your Own Choosing: Beverly Ryle, Shank Painter Publishing, 2008

Grow Yourself a Life You'll Love: Barbara Garro, M.A. 2000, Thomas More, an RCL Company

Happy for No Reason: Marci Shimoff (w/carol Kline), Free Press, 2008

My Next Phase: The Personality-Based Guide to Your Best Retirement; Authors: Eric Sundstrom, PhD., Randy Burnham, Ph.D., and Michael Burnham, 2007, Springboard Press

Prime Time: (How Baby Boomers will revolutionize retirement): Marc Freedman, 1999

Retire Retirement—Career Strategies for the Boomer Generation: Tamara Erickson, 2008, Harvard Business Press, Boston, MA

Retirement On A Shoestring: John Howells, The Globe Pequot Press, 2000
Staying Sharp: Quality of Life: AARP Andrus Foundation and the Dana Alliance for Brain Initiatives (2002). Free download or booklet: "http://www. aarp.org" www.aarp.org

The New Retirement—The Ultimate Guide to The Rest of Your Life: Jan Cullinane and Cathy Fitzgerald, Holtzbrinck Publishers, 2004
The Single Woman's Guide to Retirement, Jan Cullinane, 2012

The Third Act: Reinvesting Yourself After Retirement: Edgar M. Bronfman and Catherine Whitney, G.P. Putnam, 2002

You Can Do It!: Johathan D. Pond; 2007; HarperCollins

Volunteer Vacation: Authors: Bill McMillion, Doug Cutchins, and Anne Geissinger, 8th Edition 2003 with forward by Ed Asner

Volunteer Vacations Across America: Sheryl Kayne, The Countryman Press/ WW Norton Co. 2009

What Color is Your Parachute? For Retirement: Authors: Richard N. Bolles and John E. Nlson, 2007

CATEGORIZED LIST OF VOLUNTEER ORGANIZATIONS

NOTE: for research information SEARCH: www.CharityNavigator.org

Communication
AARP
Administration on Aging
Discovering What's Next
Life Planning Network

Community
Boomer Blog (Boomthis!)
Habitat for Humanity
Junior Achievement
KABOOM
PET=Personal Energy
Transportation
Points of Light Foundation
Project H.O.M.E.
Salvation Army
Volunteer Match

Environment
American Hiking Society
Barbados Sea Turtle Project
Earthwatch Institute
Environmental Alliance for Senior
Involvement
Global Genie
Global Service Corps
Globe Aware
Greater Good
Hawthorne Valley Farm
Heifer International
JAARS
Marine Life (Merrin Institute)
Nature Conservancy (by State)

Organic Farm Volunteers
Reef Relief
SEEDS (Iceland)
Sierra Club
Sunbow Farm
Volunteer Louisiana
WWOFF USA

Faith-Based
CNVS-Catholic Network of Vol
Service
Episcopal Church
Ghost Ranch
Holden Village
Mennonite Central Committee
National Parks, Christian Ministry
National Retiree Vol Coalition
National Senior Service Corps
Presbyterian Church
Simply Smiles
Spring Lake Ranch
Stony Point Conference Center
UCC-United Church of Christ
Warren Wilson College
YMCA of the Rockies

Government
AmeriCorps
Ask a Friend Campaign
CNS-Corporation for National and
Community Service
Ed M Kennedy Serve America Act
(see AmeriCorps)

Experience Corps
Military (access by State)
National Audubon Society (by State)
National Tropical Botanical Garden
National Parks (by State/Location)
Peace Corps
Red Cross
Senior Corps (The)
VISTA

Health
Alzheimer's Association
Dept of Health & Human Services
Educational Cruises
Real Age
Senior Friend Finder
Silver Sneakers
Your Disease Risk

Housing
4homeex
Best Places
Caretaker Gazette
Couch Surfing
Cruise Ship Condos
Educational Cruises
Find Your Spot
Rebuilding Together
RPITA-Recreational Trailer Assoc.
Senior Co-housing

International
Cross Cultural Solutions
Workaway International

Travel/Vacation
Fly-for-Good
Adventure for Women

Volunteer (generic)
For each state: SEARCH individual state, enter category i.e. parks, education, with housing, etc.
For National Parks: SEARCH nps.gov

Wildlife
Arnold's Wildlife & Butterfly Haven
Bird Rescue
Humane Society (by State)

Women
Adventure for Women
Red Hat Society
Sew Much Comfort
Stonecroft Ministries
Transition Network (The)
WomanSage
Women Traveling Alone
WowOwow

A-Z LISTING OF WEBSITES
(Disclaimer: websites valid at time of publication)
NOTE: Current practice eliminates "www". Each website is current as of
publication. To verify an organization or charity try: CharityNavigator.org

4HOMEEX
freehomeawayfromhome.com
Home exchange. Offers listings with membership. Alternative to volunteer
housing.

AARP
aarp.org
Nation's largest aging organization. Volunteer, service, and employment
programs; local or global. See AARP's Day of Service.

ADMINISTRATION ON AGING
aoa.gov
Older American Act and aging network.

ADVENTURE FOR WOMEN
adventurewomen.com
Educational and adventure travel catering to women. Cost involved.

ALZHEIMER'S ASSOCIATION
alz.org
Compassion to care. Local volunteers.

AMERICAN HIKING SOCIETY
americanhiking.org
Nat'l organization dedicated to promoting and protecting US hiking trails
and natural areas. Utilizes volunteer workers for trail maintenance &
awareness.

AMERICORPS

americorps.org

Team based, national service initiative; ages 18-24, with no upper age limits. Three programs: AmeriCorps (State and National), AmeriCorps VISTA, and AmeriCorps National Civilian Community Corps (NCCC).

AMIZADE

amizade.org

Global service learning. Encourages intercultural exploration and understanding through community-driven volunteer programs at home/ abroad.

ARNOLD'S WILDLIFE REHABILITATION CENTER AND BUTTERFLY HAVEN

arnoldswildlife.org

Arnold's Wildlife Rehabilitation Center, Inc (AWRC), non-profit educational-based wildlife care facility, dedicated to awareness. Does not provide housing; local opportunities.

ASK A FRIEND CAMPAIGN

volunteerfriends.org

Developed by Senior Corps for community challenges.

AUDUBON SOCIETY

audubon.org

Conserve/restore natural ecosystems with focus on birds. Some room and board with host family. Check project costs/registration fees. Click: *take action* or Search for: *volunteer*

BARBADOS SEA TURTLE PROJECT

barbadosseaturtles.org

Recover marine turtle populations thru use of conservation measures. 2-mo stint, typically students or Biologists. Check costs/housing/work schedule.

BEST PLACES (ALSO SEARCH: WWW.TOPRETIREMENTS.COM)
bestplaces.net
Interactive site; options for where to live during retirement.

BIG BROTHERS BIG SISTERS
bbbsa.org
Mission: help children reach their potential through professionally supported, one-on-one relationships. Local opportunities.

BIRD RESCUE (BIRD SANCTUARY)
saveourseabirds.org
Starting point for bird rescue, rehabilitate, and release.

BOOMER WEBSITE (ALSO SEARCH: BOOMTHIS.BLOGSPOT.COM)
boomthis.com
Your link to all things Boomer.

BRIDGES
oneworld365.org
Building Responsible International Dialogue through Grassroots Exchanges. See also: Volunteer Match.

CAMPHILL SPECIAL SCHOOL (WALDORF SCHOOL, PA)
smartvolunteer.org
Create wholeness for youth with developmental disabilities through education. Volunteers help with large projects. Resident and non-resident opportunities. Access menu: Volunteer

CARETAKER GAZETTE
caretaker@caretaker.org
Caretaker opportunities in the U.S. and abroad. Check cost for membership and travel. Volunteer and paid options.

COUNCIL OF INTERNATIONAL PROGRAMS (CIP)
ciee.org
Council of International Programs USA (CIPUSA): non-profit international educational exchange program promoting international understanding and cross-cultural exchange. Check costs.

CLEARWATER (HUDSON RIVER SLOOP CLEARWATER)
clearwater.org
Conducts environmental education/advocacy programs to protect the Hudson River. Volunteers serve one week on the sloop. Check costs.

COUCH SURFING
couchsurfing.org
Volunteer-based worldwide network connecting travelers with members of local communities who offer free accommodation and/or advice. Check costs.

CNVS
catholicvolunteernetwork.org
Catholic Network of Volunteer Service: national membership organization fosters national/ international service opportunities. Website has search response directory.

CORPORATION FOR NATIONAL AND COMMUNITY SERVICE (CNS)
nationalservice.gov
CNS functions as umbrella for many national service programs; serves/ operates the National Senior Service Corps, Experience Corps for Independent Living.

CROSS-CULTURAL SOLUTIONS (ALSO SEARCH: *internationalvolunteer. org*)
crossculturalsolutions.org
International non-profit organization supporting local short-term projects. Year-round dates, 1-12 weeks, all ages and abilities. Check costs.

CRUISE SHIP CONDOS
itotd.com/articles/576/cruise-ship-condos/
Alternative living on the sea at a cost. Also SEARCH: cruise ship condos.

DEPARTMENT OF HEALTH AND HUMAN SERVICES
www.hhs.gov (Note: must use *www.hhs.gov* to access appropriate website.)
Site dedicated to improving health, safety, and well-being of all Americans.
See site to access health information for age 65+. (Admin on Aging)

DISCOVERING WHAT'S NEXT
discoveringwhatsnext.com
Network of people and community organizations that connects individuals
50+ to inspire and support fostering action to benefit communities.

EARTHWATCH INSTITUTE
earthwatch.org
Supports scientific field research, offering opportunities to join research
teams home & abroad attempting to change how the public views the role
of science in environmental sustainability.

EDUCATIONAL TRAVEL IN THE U.S. (ROAD SCHOLAR)
roadscholar.org/programs/usa.asp
Non-profit organization providing lifelong learning at home/abroad to
adults aged fifty-five and over. Associated with Elderhostel. Program costs.

EDWARD M. KENNEDY SERVE AMERICA ACT
americorps.gov
Expansion of AmeriCorps, a domestic service program, 10% are slots for
volunteers over 55. Investigate fellowships; scholarships for continuing
education. Affiliated with AARP.

EMPTY NEST MOMS
emptynestmoms.com
A community of female empty nesters for networking and camaraderie.
Blogs, advice, Q&A.

ENCORE CAREERS (ALSO SEARCH: LIFE PLANNING NETWORK
LIFEPLANNINGNETWORK.ORG)
encore.org
Find out about purpose-filled careers in the second half of life.

ENVIRONMENTAL ALLIANCE FOR SENIOR INVOLVEMENT
easi.org
Volunteers in Senior Environment Corps™ (SEC) organizations in every state and 20 foreign countries carry out a wide range of environmental activities.

EPISCOPAL PARTNERSHIP FOR GLOBAL MISSION (ALSO SEARCH:
OURLITTLEROSES.ORG)
spiscopalchurch.org
Enables Episcopalians to participate in God's global mission, domestic and foreign.

EXPERIENCE CORPS
www.experiencecorps.org
New adventures in service for Americans over fifty-five.

EXPERIENCE WORKS
experienceworks.org
Employment training for low-income seniors.

FIND YOUR SPOT
findyourspot.com
A quiz to help you find the best place for you to live.

FLY FOR GOOD
flyforgood.org
Discounted airfare for volunteers.

Generations United
gu.org

National membership organization focused on improving the lives of children, youth, and older people through intergenerational strategies, programs and public policy.

Geographic Expeditions
geoex.com

Travel to remote and challenging destinations. Varied portfolio of overland tours/treks/walks/voyages home/abroad. Program costs.

Ghost Ranch
ghostranch.org (Also SEARCH: pcusa.org)

Affiliate of Presbyterian Church (www.pcusa.org). Two locations: Ghost Ranch Conference Center in Santa Fe and Abiquiu, NM. Both offer long/short term opportunities. Housing for long-term.

Globe Aware
globeaware.org

Short-term programs to promote cultural awareness & sustainability in South America and Asia. Check costs.

Global Genie
greentravel.org

Interactive site fostering global movement towards a just society dedicated to helping people find opportunity to undertake socially conscious travel. Click on "volunteer links" in menu.

Global Neighbour Network
Nabuur.com

Global volunteer site where online neighbors are matched with local communities. Costs involved.

GLOBAL SERVICE CORPS
globalservicecorps.org
Volunteer programs and International Internships in Thailand, Cambodia
& Tanzania. Check costs.

GLOBAL VOLUNTEERS
globalvolunteers.org
Facilitates short-term (up to 24 weeks) service for community-dev programs
in host communities abroad. Program fees/ costs.

GREATER GOOD
greatergood.com
On-line charity working to protect the health and well-being of people,
animals and the planet.

HABITAT FOR HUMANITY INTERNATIONAL
habitat.org
Non-profit, non-denominational Christian housing organization home and
abroad. Check site for program/travel costs.

HAWAII RETREAT CENTER
kalani.com
Hawaiian Oceanside retreat. One to three month commitment; shared
housing. Tuition fee.

HAWTHORNE VALLEY FARM
Hawthornevalleyfarm.com
Local sustainable living and farming work in NY. Access site for Internship
information.

HEIFER INTERNATIONAL
heifer.org
Non-profit organization working to end world hunger. Helps communities
become self-reliant. Access site to complete volunteer application. Long/
short term opportunities in MA and AR.

Holden Village (state of WA)
holdenvillage.org
Year-round retreat center accepts long/short term volunteers of all faiths under auspices of the Lutheran Church. Spanish spoken. Click: "work at Holden". Contact Staff Coordinator.

How to Live Your Dream of Volunteering Overseas
volunteeroverseas.org
Book. Information on how you can help by volunteering overseas while exploring culture, making friends, investigating yourself, and enhancing your skills. Cost.

Humane Society
hsus.org
Nations largest animal protection agency. Local opportunities.

Idealist
idealist.org
Global clearinghouse of non-profit and volunteer resources. Project of Action without Borders, founded in 1995. Offices in the U.S. and Argentina. Interactive site.

JAARS
jaars.org
Linguistics training school providing bible translation/literacy worldwide. Check costs.

Junior Achievement
ja.org
Local hands-on experience to teach adolescents the economics of life; opens minds to potential.

KABOOM
kaboom.org
National non-profit working with communities to plan new play-space in their local area.

LPN (LIFE PLANNING NETWORK)
lifeplanningnetwork.org
Community of professionals from diverse disciplines dedicated to helping people navigate the second half of life.

LITTLE ROSES MINISTRIES
ourlittleroses.org
Headquartered in Honduras. Long and short term opportunities with housing. Investigate cost.

LOCAL VOLUNTEER OPPORTUNITIES
yourstate.com/volunteer
Numerous opportunities local and long-distance. SEARCH name of individual state.

MENAUL SCHOOL
menaulschool.org
Also through www.pcusa.org. Private secondary school; grades 6-12 for a socially and economically diverse student body. Long and short term opportunities.

MENNONITE CENTRAL COMMITTEE
mcc.org/serve
Singles/married/couples; home and abroad. Check costs.

MARINE MAMMALS .... MERRIN INSTITUTE
merrinstitute.org
Marine mammals and sea turtles of Delaware. Volunteer to help protect 30 species of marine life.

Military
legion.org
Clip coupons for military families. Contact American Legion Auxiliary for clipping, organizing and mailing coupons to needy military families.

National Tropical Botanical Garden
ntbg.org
Tropical plant research. Committed to building and nurturing natural resources. Ages 14 to 90+. Orientation and on-the-job training specific to positions. Click : "How you can Help"

National Audubon Society
audubon.org
Conserve and restore natural ecosystems. Local volunteer opportunities.

National Parks
www.nationalparks.gov www.volunteer.gov
Interactive site. Select park on drop-down menu. Complete forms/submit.

National Parks: Christian Ministry
acmnp.com
Year-round ministry interactive site for government personnel and families in park areas.

National Senior Service Corps
cns.gov
National Senior Service Corps engages 55+ and older Americans in service efforts in all fifty states.

Nature Conservancy
nature.org
Dedicated to help nature and the environment. Interactive site.

OLDER AMERICANS ACT PROGRAMS
eldercare.gov
Various local opportunities.

OLDER WOMEN'S LEAGUE (OWL)
owl-national.org
Grassroots organization for women as they age. Stresses quality of life.

ONE-WAY TRIPS (TRAVEL BY AUTO OR RV)
autodriveaway.com or *cruiseamerica.com* or *elmonterv.com*
Check on-line for particulars.

OPERATION PLAYGROUND
operationplayground.org
Initiative to build playgrounds in areas affected by weather/trauma. See also KABOOM.

ORGANIC FARM VOLUNTEERS
wwoofusa.org
Short/long term opportunities working at more than 400 farms and homestead across the U.S. in exchange for harvesting crops. Possible room/board. Research details. Membership costs.

OUR LITTLE ROSES
ourlittleroses.org
San Pedro Sula, Honduras (affiliated with the Episcopal Church).

OVER FIFTIES
overfifties.com
Bulletin board and chat room for 50+ adults.

PEACE CORPS
peacecorps.gov
Federal agency devoted to world peace/friendship. Lengthy application process; 3 month orientation; 26-month commitment. Interactive site.

PET (Personal Energy Transportation)
petinternational.org
Help manufacture hand-cranked, three-wheeled, sturdy and maintainable wheelchair for those disabled by war or illness. Check personal cost involved.

Points of Light Foundation
pointsoflight.org
Foundation works in U.S. to promote volunteering and service. Informational site.

Presbyterian Church
pcusa.org
Interactive site lists opportunities for local and long/short term volunteering. Search: volunteer.

Project H.O.M.E.
projecthome.org
Mission: to empower adults, children, and families to break cycle of poverty. Local opportunities.

Real Age
realage.com
Interesting interactive site to explore the real age of your body.

Rebuilding Together
rebuildingtogether.org
Nonprofit working to preserve affordable homeownership and revitalize communities. Local.

Red Cross
redcross.org
Interactive site offering opportunities for long/short term volunteering. Check personal cost.

RED HAT SOCIETY
redhatsociety.com
Global society of women that supports and encourages women.

REEF RELIEF
reefrelief.org
Coral reef conservation program. Visit site. E-mail with specific interest. Check costs.

RETIREMENT BOOT CAMP
kripalu.org
Weekend seminar each year at Kripalu Center, Stockbridge, MA. Search: retirement. Check costs.

ROTARY CLUBS
rotary.org
Civic organization focusing on local philanthropic efforts. Google: town/ city.

RPTIA (RECREATIONAL PARK TRAILER INDUSTRY ASSOCIATION
rptia.com
400-sq foot movable resort cottage designed exclusively recreational use.

SALVATION ARMY
salvationarmyusa.org
Interactive U.S. and international site providing volunteer opportunities.

SEEDS
seedsiceland.org
Promotes environment protection; long/short volunteer opportunities. Check housing and costs.

SENIOR CORP OF RETIRED EXECUTIVES (SCORE)

score.org

Association of retired local businessmen/women who consult with nonprofit/public service agencies.

SENIOR COHOUSING

seniorcohousing.com

Communal living in community housing.

SENIOR CORPS

seniorcorps.gov

National network of projects to place "seniors" in local volunteer assignments.

SENIOR VOLUNTEERS

seniorcorps.gov/about/programs/rsvp.asp

Provides local service opportunities through RSVP.

SEW MUCH COMFORT

sewmuchcomfort.org

Provides free adaptive clothing for unique needs of injured service members from all branches of the military and national guard. Local and nationwide.

SIERRA CLUB

sierraclub.org

Interactive site of the oldest, largest, environmental organization.

SILVER SNEAKERS

silver sneakers.com

Interactive site for preventative exercise (perk for those over 65).

SIMPLY SMILES

www.simplysmiles.org

Mission work in Mexico. Access site for information on programs/costs.

SPRING LAKE RANCH, RUTLAND, VT
springlakeranch.org
Therapeutic community program utilizing volunteers. Call for particulars.

STONECROFT MINISTRIES
stonecroft.org
Christian ministry site for women who wish to help locally through outreach ministries.

STONY POINT CONFERENCE CENTER, NY
pcusa.org
Affiliated with the Presbyterian Church. Access through www.pcusa.org. Search: volunteer

SUNBOW FARM (OR)
sunbowfarm.org
Organic farm utilizing local volunteers. Contact directly.

TRANSITION NETWORK (THE)
thetransitionnetwork.org (TTN)
TNN is a vibrant community of NYC women facing transition by taking control of their lives.

UNITED CHURCH OF CHRIST (Also:YASC ages 21-31/Summer Communities of Service ages 19-30)
ucc.org
Partner with local agencies. Search: volunteer. See also

UNITED NATIONS VOLUNTEERS
unv.org
Interactive site providing on-line volunteer opportunities at home and abroad. Check costs.

UNITED PLANET

unitedplanet.org

Interactive site offers unique short/long-term international volunteer programs. Check personal cost.

USA FREEDOM CORPS

serve.gov

Service opportunities to match individual interests and talents. National and community service.

VIRTUAL VOLUNTEER

volunteermatch.org

Allows contribution of skills from "virtually anywhere". People matched to causes on-line.

VISTA

americorps.org/about/programs/vista.asp

An affiliate of AmeriCorps.

VOCATION VACATIONS

VocationVacations.com

Unique opportunity to test-drive career change. Check costs.

VOLUNTEER OVERSEAS AND LEARN A LANGUAGE

projects-abroad.org

British service organization combines volunteer work in developing areas with classroom instruction in one of 18 languages. Check program/travel costs.

VOLUNTEERS OF AMERICA

voa.org

Investigative site for volunteer opportunities.

VOLUNTEER "ANYWHERE" - OR VOLUNTEER OKLAHOMA, AUSTRALIA, ETC.

volunteeringANYWHERE.org

Place the name of a U.S. state or foreign country within address line to access a site of interest.

VOLUNTER IN A SPECIFIC PLACE w/HOUSING

volunteerinyourdestination.org (place your destination in address line)

Older American Act and aging network.

VOLUNTEER OVERSEAS

volunteeroverseas.org

BOOK: options for volunteering abroad.

VOLUNTEERS IN PARKS (FOR NATIONAL USE NPS.ORG/ FOR STATE, GOOGLE INDIVIDUALLY)

nps.org

See also National Park Service

WOMENSAGE

womensage.org

WomanSage provides support for women in midlife through education and social philanthropy.

WOMEN TRAVELING ALONE

www.smartertravel.com *www.women-traveling.com*

Anxious about solo travel? Access this site.

WORK-CAMPING

workamper.com

PT seasonal options at resorts, theme parks or towns. RVers welcome.

WORKAWAY INTERNATIONAL

workaway.com

Recruitment company providing employment in the U.S.

WowOwow

www.wowOwow.com (Women on the Web)

Manhattan based Executive Intern program. Click on "Think Up!".

WWOOF USA

wwoofusa.org

Organic farmers promote educational exchange/global community consciousness utilizing volunteer pickers in fields. Check housing. Research individual project cost and location.

YMCA OF THE ROCKIES

ymcarockies.org

Affordable family and group destinations. Conference center volunteer opportunities exchanging skills for room and board. Variety of interests and skill levels.

YOUR DISEASE RISK

vitals.com

Check your risk for disease on-line.

Index

Made in the USA
Lexington, KY
08 June 2013